FINTAN O'TOOLE

THE POLITICS OF PAIN

POSTWAR ENGLAND AND THE RISE OF NATIONALISM

LIVERIGHT PUBLISHING CORPORATION

A DIVISION OF W. W. NORTON & COMPANY

Independent Publishers Since 1923

New York   London

Contents

Preface: The Importance of Not Being Earnest   vii

Introduction   xv

1. The Pleasures of Self-Pity   1

2. SS-GB: Life in Occupied England   25

3. The Triumph of the Light Brigade   63

4. A Pint of Beer, a Packet of Prawn
   Cocktail Flavour Crisps and Two Ounces
   of Dog Shit, Please   93

5. Sadopopulism   121

6. The Twilight of the Gods:
   English Dreamtime   151

7. The Sore Tooth and the Broken Umbrella   173

8. Postscript: A Special Place in Hell   201

Notes   217

To Bjørn Oisín and all the new Europeans

The fact is that, in spite of the way we behave, we cannot any longer feel that the infliction of pain is merely funny

GEORGE ORWELL, 1944

PREFACE

THE IMPORTANCE OF NOT BEING EARNEST

I n her classic study, *Watching the English*, published in 2004 and updated a decade later, the social anthropologist Kate Fox wrote of her compatriots that 'the kind of hand-on-heart, gushing earnestness and pompous, Bible-thumping solemnity favoured by almost all American politicians would never win a single vote in this country'.[1] The English, she claimed, watched such American demagogues on the TV news 'with a kind of smugly detached amusement, wondering how the cheering crowds can possibly be so credulous as to fall for this sort of nonsense . . . such shamefully earnest platitudes, in such ludicrously solemn tones?' Fox proposed that all public discourse in England must observe what she called 'The Importance of Not Being Earnest Rule'.

Yet, just two years after the revised version of *Watching the English* appeared, English political life came to be dominated by shamefully earnest platitudes about national destiny uttered in ludicrously solemn tones. After June 2016, when the English heartlands of the United Kingdom voted to leave the European Union, all that smugly detached amusement seemed fatally misplaced. The English had thought of themselves as peculiarly immune to the delusions of cheering, credulous crowds. Other people (especially Americans) might be suckers for sententious appeals to an imagined national exceptionalism, but the English were protected by a force field of ironic self-deprecation. Their sense of humour was not just a form of amusement – it was also a way to keep political passions in proportion, to cut dangerously grandiose ideas down to size.

One might therefore conclude that the great crisis of English identity that came to the surface in 2016 is essentially a sense-of-humour failure. The dikes of detached amusement that had kept all forms of political extremism at bay had somehow been breached and in rushed a wave of gushing earnestness about England's special place in the world. This was certainly the case – a solemn appeal to a unique national destiny was now shaping political life. But things were much stranger than that. For The Importance of Not Being Earnest rule was not really broken. Even as the country set its face towards one of the most radical disruptions in its modern history, it could not bring itself to do so earnestly. Things were desperate but not serious – not serious enough, at least, for this great departure to be properly planned, responsibly negotiated or efficiently implemented.

If, as is often said, comedy is tragedy plus time, Fox observed in her study that the time required for the English to turn tragedy into humour is 'about a nanosecond'.[2] And, one might add, vice versa: a delightfully anarchic sense of humour, as I suggest in this book, is one of the sources of the political anarchy that took hold in England after 2016. Karl Marx claimed that everything in history happens twice – the first time as tragedy, the second as farce. But in this great national crisis, the two states were simultaneous rather than sequential: there was barely a nanosecond between them. And to understand how this could be, we have to enter into a collective frame of mind in which self-deprecation and self-aggrandisement are not opposites. They are conjoined twins.

Fox wrote of the wonderfully wacky opening ceremony for the 2012 Olympics in London that 'The degree of self-mockery, self-denigration, obscure self-reference and self-indulgent eccentricity exhibited in that ceremony required a breathtaking disregard for the opinion of others – in this case, billions of others – which can only stem from a deep sense of superiority.'[3] In the years after she wrote those words, they became a perfect description of another set of games hosted in England. The strange spectacle of Brexit would show the world how a country previously admired for its apparent equanimity could so paradoxically denigrate and mock itself in pursuit of an elusive sense of superiority.

The near-implosion of British politics after 2016 was obviously a local variant of a wider crisis of democracy. As Donald Trump Jr wrote in March 2019, 'In a way, you could say that Brexit and my father's election are one and the same'[4] – the same rhetoric of the people versus the elites was deployed using the same dark arts of mass persuasion. It is equally obvious that the stunning result of the Brexit referendum was merely the most dramatic expression of a much wider sense of alienation in Europe. The long years of budgetary austerity after the great banking crisis of 2008, gross inequalities in the division of the spoils of economic globalization and the huge wave of refugees from the catastrophic collapse of Syria created a potent cocktail of popular anxieties. Across most of Europe, the reactionary Right has both fed and been fed by those anxieties. The old coalitions of Social Democrats and Christian Democrats struggled almost everywhere to maintain their footing on a centre ground that was rapidly narrowing. White identity politics filled the vacuum where the promise of incremental progress had once been.

It makes perfect sense, then, to see what happened in England as a local version of a global phenomenon, just one eruption on a great seismic fault line that stretches across the continents. But it is also different. For one thing, the English continued to vote – both before the Brexit referendum in the general election of 2015 and after it in the election of 2017 – for their traditional political parties. In England, 88 per cent of voters cast their ballots in 2017 for either the Conservatives or Labour, and this long-established duopoly won all but nine of the 533 English parliamentary seats. More strangely, those who led what was in effect a peaceful revolution in 2016, could not actually take power. The insurgent United Kingdom Independence Party (UKIP), which, under its former leader Nigel Farage created the demand for the referendum, actually lost virtually all of its vote in 2017. The leading Brexiteers in the ruling Conservative Party – most notably Boris Johnson – were unable to assume control of government, leaving it instead to the lackluster Theresa May, who had played no significant role in the referendum. There is something both very odd and highly distinctive about this – a revolution at once triumphant and timid, boldly self-assertive in principle but in practice tentative and hesitant to the point, ultimately, of complete paralysis.

This peculiar continuity amidst the upheavals is in one sense easily explained: antipathy to 'Europe' displaced the anti-Establishment anger that England shared with the US and other countries away from the indigenous Establishment and onto 'Brussels'. This might even be seen as in one sense a brilliantly self-protective act by a ruling class that anticipated the coming wave of rage but channelled it away from its own shores. This, however, begs a key question – why did this deflection work? How was it possible to convince a majority of voters that they needed to be liberated – not from their actual rulers but from an imagined prison-house of European regulation?

To put it mildly, the Brexiteers, when placed under the pressure of making their dream project a reality, did not emerge as political geniuses. They were effective, surely, not because they had a superb plan but because Brexit was a drilling-down into the half-buried layers of a very distinctive English mindset. It hit pay dirt, and out gushed a flow of feelings highly specific to the mental terrain of post-war England. The most potent of them is a feeling that it was just not right for England to be a normal European country, that there is something amiss with an arrangement in which it appears to be just one prosperous, privileged Western European democracy among all the others. As the chief secretary to the Treasury and ardent Brexiteer Liz

Truss tweeted in April 2019, 'We are not an ordinary country. We're an extraordinary country.' The 'ex' in Brexit also stands for 'exceptional', and what is exceptional about Britain is that it won the Second World War but almost immediately lost an empire. It is to the strange consequences of these closely related aspects of its modern history that we must turn for an explanation both of Brexit's imaginative appeal and of its inability to function as a real political project. Its power and its impotence have the same roots in the history and culture of post-war England.

The great upheaval after 2016 was never really about Europe. Those who caused it turned out to have very little interest in, and consequently very little knowledge of, the EU itself. They did not understand how the EU would negotiate as a collective or how seriously it would take its own rules or how it would prioritize political necessities over economic discomforts. They had no plan for how the UK would relate to the EU after Brexit, largely because that relationship was not the real focus of their obsessions. They were concerned, in reality, with Britain's relationship to itself and to its own self-image. Their desire was to exit a condition of ordinariness which, they had succeeded in convincing themselves, is an unnatural and oppressive imposition on an extraordinary country.

This sense of oppression is imaginary, and it is the imaginative world from which it arose that is the subject of this book. But I also suggest that the indulgence of this masochistic pleasure created a demented variety of wish-fulfilment: its perverse magic was to make real the very conditions that were conjured as dark fantasies. The bedrock assumption was that England was humiliated by being in the EU – and it actually humiliated itself on the world stage through its inability to organize a coherent departure from the EU. It was driven by a profound sense of self-pity – it produced a genuinely pitiable image of a British polity in a state of near-collapse. It evoked the EU as a bureaucratic monster but itself became a nightmare of bureaucratic tedium in which politics came to be dominated by obscure technicalities. It wallowed in the notion that England had become a colony of the EU but then led the country towards the real possibility that it would end up as a mere satellite of the EU, not part of its decision-making process but unable to escape its orbit.

The route to such irrational outcomes cannot be entirely rational. It must run through a strange and dark terrain that, on the mental maps of a very particular reactionary discourse, is called England.

INTRODUCTION

London that summer had a sort of heat I'd never experienced in Ireland, the dense, closed-in kind you get only in very big cities. It was 1969, I was eleven years old and this was my first day in England. I'd come over on the boat from Dublin to Liverpool with my father and my brother, who was thirteen. We'd come on the bus through the English Midlands, a deeply foreign landscape of motorways and service stations and giant power plants. My father's first cousin Vincent had met us at the terminus and we'd taken another bus across to the East End, where we'd be staying with my mother's sister Brigid. Brigid was a nun, so we were actually going to be staying in a Catholic convent. Between the heat and the prospect of three days behind convent walls, my dad decided he could do with a pint. So my brother and myself were left sitting on a low wall with bottles of Fanta, while Vincent and my father disappeared into the pub.

I remember sitting on that wall and sucking on the straw to try to suppress a rising panic. We were alone in England, abandoned in an alien place. England, as an idea, terrified me. I knew from history lessons in school that the English only ever did bad things to Irish people. And I knew that the heart of that badness was Protestant. There was one true faith, which was, of course, Catholic, so England by its very nature was deviant. You wouldn't know what to expect of such people – except that it would not be nice. My older brother was playing it cool. I was sweating with heat and inherited anxiety.

Then, along the road, came an enormous man in flowing white robes, his height accentuated by a tall leopard-skin hat. He had an entourage of five or six men, also dressed in white but far less flamboyant. He was surely some kind of dignitary, a minor king perhaps or a tribal chief. I couldn't help staring at him. He held my gaze and his face lit up with a huge smile. He patted me on the head in a gesture of blessing and benevolence and said something to his sidekicks in a language I did not recognize. He looked down at me and asked, 'Are you enjoying your pop?' Pop wasn't a word we used in Ireland for sugary drinks, but I knew what it meant. I knew from the British comics we devoured, the *Beano* and the *Dandy*, that it was something English kids said. And it struck me that he thought my brother and myself were natives, that we were English. I was quite indignant. I wanted to explain to him that he had it all wrong, that we were visitors at least as foreign as himself. But I was too awestruck to say anything and in any case he was sailing majestically onwards down the street, trailed by the brilliant white wake of his entourage.

I've sometimes wondered what my eleven-year-old self might have said to that regal personage if I could have articulated any of my feelings. What if he had heard my protests and dismissed them: 'Well you look English to me, so why all the fuss?' What if he'd asked what we were doing here anyway? I'd have had to tell him that my uncle Vincent, who was in the pub behind us, had left working-class Dublin and been able to get a great education in England, ending up at Oxford University and then as a lecturer in English at Warwick. And that we were going to stay with my auntie, the nun, who was working as a nurse in the East End. And after that we'd be going to stay in Maidstone with my father's brother Kevin, who had been a quartermaster sergeant in the Royal Engineers and voted Tory. And then we were going to stay with my mother's brother Peter and his wife Cilla in Manchester: he was a bus driver and she worked in a sewing factory and they were Labour people. And that all their kids – the cousins who spoke with a Kentish burr or a Manchester drawl – were the same as me, really, that we played the same games and watched the same TV programmes and listened to the same pop songs and got on together immediately we met because we were family. I'm not sure he'd have been convinced my Irishness was anything more than a tiny local variation of Englishness.

It was much more, of course – and it still is. Being Irish isn't something you have to prove – it's just a matter of fact. But it's also not simple and in particular it is not what my eleven-year-old self thought it was – the opposite of being English. Relationships within what we now call 'these islands' are fluid, ambiguous and complex. England, Scotland, Wales, Northern Ireland and the Republic of Ireland form some kind of matrix, but it is always shifting and never stable. And the people who belong within these entities are not simple or stable either. We let identities go and we bring them back from the dead.

Sometimes, the network of relationships matters a lot and sometimes we forget about it because we are too busy looking inwards. Most of the time, we are quite comfortable holding at least two contradictory ideas in our heads at the same time.

I grew up with those contradictions. The official Irish culture of my childhood and youth was one that defined Ireland as whatever England was not. England was Protestant; so Catholicism had to be the essence of Irish identity. England was industrial; so Ireland had to make a virtue of its under-developed and deindustrialized economy. England was urban; so Ireland had to create an image of itself that was exclusively rustic. The English were scientific rationalists; so we Irish had to be the mystical dreamers of dreams. They were Anglo-Saxons; we were Celts. They had a monarchy, so we had to have a republic. They developed a welfare state; so we relied on the tender mercies of charity. In other words, I know exactly what an either/or identity looks and feels like.

But life just wasn't like that. Two of my uncles and two of my aunts fought for the British during the war, and I have always been proud that they played their part in defeating fascism. My aunts and uncles were very happy to work in factories and services in English cities. They emigrated, not so much to England as to the welfare state. The Irish, like so many other migrant peoples, helped to build one of the great achievements of civilization, the National Health Service, and enjoyed its benefits. They relished the educational opportunities opened up by British social democracy. And, though they were certainly capable of racism, many also relished life in a multi-ethnic society. Many of my cousins are half-Irish and half-Afro-Caribbean or half-Irish and half-Asian. And, though Catholicism was an important point of distinction, it is also true that many Irish people preferred to live in England because they could escape from Irish sexual prejudice and repression.

Six years after that first visit to London, when I was seventeen, I spent the summer working in a huge cinema in Piccadilly Circus. It was the first place I was ever asked a particular question: 'Are you gay or straight?' I murmured almost apologetically that I was straight – apologetically because I had quickly realized that almost everyone who worked there was gay. The manager was gay and he hired gay men, so that the place was a kind of safe haven. I had been given a job on a mistaken assumption. But that was okay – I was tolerated. And it was an important, if rather ironic, experience, a tiny taste of what it's like to belong to a sexual minority. I think in different ways England did this for a lot of Irish people – it taught us how 'majority' and 'minority' are moveable feasts. In Ireland, most of us were part of a powerful majority culture; in England we had to learn what it was like to belong to the few rather than the many.

So we had these two very different ways of thinking about England: as the opposite of *Us* and as a place where *Us* could mean something much more fluid and open. And the poignant thing about the decade before the Brexit referendum of June 2016 is not that one of these ways of thinking had banished the other; it's that they've both been banished. The first one – the notion that Ireland and England are opposites – is long gone. No Irish kid today would experience the sense of strangeness in moving through a built-up English landscape that I felt in

1969: most Irish people now live in the same kind of urban or suburban places as their English counterparts do. Ireland is a lot less Catholic and England a lot less Protestant – and in any case religion matters much less to either nation's collective identity. Perhaps most importantly, England and Ireland are no longer the two opposite poles of nationality on these islands – Wales, and in particular an unsettled Scotland, are much more assertive parts of the matrix.

So the historical antagonisms I grew up with had been replaced by intense co-operation and a mutual interest in peace – it is no exaggeration to say that Anglo-Irish relations were, in the years immediately before the Brexit vote, more cordial than they had ever been in the entire tangled history of 'these islands'. The loss of this simplistic opposition is all to the good. It vanished in part because Ireland has changed. The time is long gone, for example, when Irish people had to cross the sea to experience life in a multi-cultural and multi-ethnic society – rapid inward migration since the 1990s has brought that experience home. The time is also gone when LGBT people felt they had to leave Ireland for a more accepting culture in Britain. After a referendum in 2018 overturned Ireland's ban on abortion, Irish women no longer have to travel to England to terminate pregnancies. If England is less of an escape for Irish people it is partly because there is less to escape *from*.

But things are changing for less benign reasons, too. The image of an open, tolerant England, a place of opportunity and acceptance, is not gone but, after June 2016, it has been diminishing rapidly. It is harder to know what to make of England because it is harder to guess what England makes of itself. It sometimes seems that there must be a fixed amount of anxiety about nationhood and identity in these islands – when it falls on one side of the Irish Sea, as it has done in Ireland, it rises equally on the other side.

If the oppositions we used to live with are gone, we are left with a paradox: the Irish Sea has never seemed so narrow or its two sides so alike. Yet Ireland and Britain may be about to become more separate than they have ever been, divided by a European Union border.

There was a time when many Irish people would have dreamed of this state of affairs, when fervent nationalists would have loved nothing better than to have the strongest possible barriers between Ireland and Britain. As the Irish nationalist ballad had it: 'The sea o the sea... Long may it roll between England and me... Thank God we're surrounded by water.' But now it is hard to find an Irish person who would not deeply regret it. That in itself says something. Underneath the politics, things have settled down into an ordinary decency, a largely contented neighbourliness. After so many centuries of bitterness, that is no mean feat.

The delight of Anglo-Irish relations in the decades after the Belfast Agreement was that they had finally evolved to be nicely boring. The sharing of a small space in a big world had become as normal as it should be. To each other, the English and the Irish were no big deal. But the fact of it all being no big deal was a very big deal indeed. Just because it was undramatic, we should not have let this state of affairs be taken for granted. It is hard won and it should not be lost sight of in all the madness of Brexit.

I write this by way of introduction because this book says some harsh things about the state of England. It is not intended to be unfriendly: when your neighbour is going mad it is only reasonable to want to understand the source of their distress. It is not intended to be gleeful: when a country you have such deep affection for is going through such pain, it is only right to share the anger at those who are causing it. And it is not intended to be superior: when your own country has experienced all the worst agonies that zero-sum nationalism can inflict, it is not *Schadenfreude* to hope that a country with which it is so closely intertwined can somehow yet avoid it.

This book is not an account of the process of Brexit. How could it be? Those books will be written far into the future, when the end of the story is known. I can but hope that they will read like manuals of escapology and not like autopsy reports. What I have attempted here is simply one possible answer to the most obvious question: how did a great nation bring itself to the point of such wilful self-harm? It may reasonably be objected that this is a family matter and that no outsider has the right to pry. I can but reply that as an Irish person I am a very close kind of outsider. My own country is profoundly affected by the crisis of English identity. This is our history, too.

This is not, then, a book about Britain: Scotland and Wales are largely absent because I argue that Brexit is essentially an English phenomenon. And although I sometimes have to lapse into the shortcut 'the English', it is not a description of that complex, contradictory and deeply divided people. Nor does this purport to be a profound analysis of the economic dislocations and insecurities without which English unhappiness could not have had such a dramatic result. It is merely an attempt to explore a mentality. It is a short journey into what Raymond Williams called a 'structure of feeling': the strange sense of imaginary oppression that underlies Brexit.

This mentality is by no means exclusive to the Right. There is a long leftist tradition of seeing continental slavishness as a threat to English liberty, and of imagining England as the only green and pleasant land in which the new Jerusalem could be built. A Roundhead distrust of the EU's suspiciously Catholic roots and a fierce, defiant insularity have shaped attitudes in some parts of the Left since the 1950s. It has also been convenient to think of the EU as the vector of neoliberalism, as if Thatcherism (and the failures on the Left that contributed to its ascendancy) were an unEnglish aberration. This leftist anti-Europeanism is not at the core of this book, however. It has created, in Labour's response to Brexit, only paralysis. The imaginary oppression that has helped to make things happen is primarily a phantasm of the reactionary Right and I therefore concentrate much more on its political manifestations within conservatism.

Almost all of this book is new, but it builds on what I have written about Brexit over the last four years. My main home for this work has been the *Irish Times*, one of the world's most civilized newspapers. I am deeply grateful to Paul O'Neill, John McManus, Conor Goodman and all my colleagues there. I am also indebted for the hospitality of their pages and websites to Katherine Butler at the *Guardian*, Robert Yates at the *Observer* and Matt Seaton and Ian Buruma at the *New York Review of Books*. I am also hugely indebted to Leonard and Ellen Milberg for their great support and friendship and to Natasha Fairweather and Neil Belton for responding so generously and capably to my sudden whims.

I am very grateful to Saul Dubow, Bill Schwarz and Camilla Schofield for their penetrating suggestions, though of course they bear no responsibility for anything written here. I have benefited greatly in the last stages of writing from being included in tremendously stimulating conversations led by Stuart Ward and Astrid Rasch of the University of Copenhagen's Embers of Empire project. I would especially like to thank Yasmin Khan, Olivette Odete, Richard Drayton, Katie Donnington, Richard Toye and Michael Kenny. I have, of course, no one to blame but myself for any errors of fact or interpretation.

My debt to Clare Connell is bottomless.

October 2018

1.

THE PLEASURES OF SELF-PITY

An Englishman will burn his bed to catch a flea

—TURKISH PROVERB

O f all the pleasurable emotions, self-pity is the one that most makes us want to be on our own. Since no one else can fully share it, it is best savoured in solitude. Only alone can we surrender completely to it and immerse ourselves in the steaming bath of hurt, outrage and tender regard for our terribly wronged selves. Brexit therefore makes sense for a nation that feels sorry for itself. The mystery, though, is how Britain, or more precisely England, came not just to experience this delightful sentiment but to define itself through it.

We tend to think of self-pity as being similar to low self-esteem, but it is in fact a form of self-regard. The great early nineteenth-century English radical Leigh Hunt, in his commentary on John Keats, picks up on the phrase 'flattered to tears' in the poem 'Music': 'In this word "flattered" is the whole theory of the secret of tears; which are the tributes, more or less worthy, of self-pity to self-love. Whenever we shed tears, we take pity on ourselves; and we feel, if we do not consciously say so, that we deserve to have the pity taken.'[1]

The more highly we think of ourselves, the sorrier we feel for ourselves when we do not get what we know we deserve. Herbert Spencer in *The Principles of Psychology* puzzled over the emotion he variously called 'pleasurably-painful sentiment', 'the luxury of grief', and 'self-pity':

> It seems possible that this sentiment, which makes a sufferer wish to be alone with his grief, and makes him resist all distraction from it, may arise from dwelling on the contrast between his own worth as he estimates it and the treatment he has received... If he feels he has deserved much while he has received little, and still more if instead of good there has come evil, the consciousness of this evil is qualified by the consciousness of worth, made pleasurably dominant by the contrast. One who contemplates his own affliction as undeserved necessarily contemplates his own merit... there is an idea of much withheld and a feeling of implied superiority to those who withhold it.[2]

Self-pity thus combines two things that may seem incompatible: a deep sense of grievance and a high sense of superiority. It is this doubleness that makes it so important to the understanding of Brexit, a political phenomenon that is driven by ideas that would not otherwise combine. Crudely, passionate nationalism has taken two antagonistic forms. There is an imperial nationalism and an anti-imperial nationalism; one sets out to dominate the world, the other to throw off such dominance. The incoherence of the new English nationalism that lies behind Brexit is that it wants to be both simultaneously. On the one hand, Brexit is fuelled by fantasies of 'Empire 2.0', a reconstructed global mercantilist trading empire in which the old white colonies will be reconnected to the mother country. On the other, it is an insurgency and therefore needs to imagine that it is a revolt against intolerable oppression. It therefore requires both a sense of superiority and a sense of grievance. Self-pity is the only emotion that can bring them together.

Not for nothing did the most brilliant and popular comic character of the post-war period in England, Tony Hancock, repeatedly play out three-part episodes in which his delusions of grandeur led to painful disappointment and luxurious self-pity. In 1971, around the time of the publication of the British government's White Paper proposing entry into what was then the Common Market, the English writer Colin Wilson wrote:

> Over the past twenty-five years, the English have built up a national grudge – perhaps due to disappointed expectations after winning the War – and now it is so firmly established that the country resembles one of those Strindbergian households where everybody nags and tries to make everybody else miserable. On the other hand, the Germans at the end of the War had the same advantage as Britain at the

beginning – of facing a crisis situation that left no room for resentment or petulance. The result was the German economic recovery. Meanwhile, like spoilt children, the English sit around scowling and quarrelling, and hoping for better times.[3]

This is, of course, greatly exaggerated and overly generalized. But it has a grain of truth. Britain was entitled to a national grudge. As Arnold Toynbee reflected in 1962, 'The consciousness of having once been heroes can be as great a handicap as the consciousness of having once failed to rise to the occasion.'[4] Britain had, after all, been on the winning side in the continent's two great twentieth-century wars. And if the mythology of the 'finest hour' and of 'standing alone' in the early part of the Second World War was overdone, there had indeed been extraordinary resolve, ingenuity and heroism in 1940 during the Battle of Britain and afterwards in North Africa, Italy and northern Europe. It was by no means ridiculous to feel that Britain, in Spencer's terms, had deserved much but received little. It had lost its empire, become virtually bankrupt, suffered economic stagnation and, in the Suez Crisis of 1956 (just over a decade after the great triumph), had its pretensions as a world power brutally exposed. To make matters much worse, the former Axis powers of Japan, Germany and Italy were booming, as were France and the Benelux countries, all of whom had been rescued from the Nazis in part by the British. Who could avoid a sense of disappointed expectations?

We must acknowledge, too, the sheer exhilaration of being English for a young, white, privileged man during and after the war. In 1962, when Britain was making its first abortive bid to join the Common Market, the journalist and historian of the British Empire James (later Jan) Morris recalled the euphoria of those years. When he turned nineteen, he was given a commission in a "superb" cavalry regiment in 'one of the most triumphant armies of British history.' His comrades were 'men of remarkable character, cultivation, and assurance' in a division that had fought its way triumphantly across North Africa and up through Italy: 'Our enemies were humbled, our allies seemed dullards beside us, and it never occurred to me to doubt that this intensely English organism, this amalgam of bravado and tradition . . . was the very best thing of its kind that any country in the world could offer.'[5]

When the six countries of the Coal and Steel Community met at Messina on 7 November 1955 – a meeting that would lead to the signing of the Treaty of Rome and the foundation of what would become the European Union – Britain was invited to join them. It sent a minor official, Russell Bretherton, under-secretary of the Board of Trade. He sat in cold silence through the meeting, then rose and delivered his verdict:

> The future treaty which you are discussing has no chance of being agreed; if it was agreed it has no chance of being ratified; and if it were ratified, it would have no chance of being applied. And if it was applied, it would be totally unacceptable to Britain. You speak of agriculture which we don't like, of power over customs, which we take exception to, and institutions, which frighten us. *Monsieur le president, messieurs, au revoir et bonne chance.*[6]

It is easy, in retrospect, to mock this blinkered arrogance, but it has a certain magnificence. It preserves the swagger of victory – a victory, moreover, that was one, not of mere imperial conquest, but of human salvation. And yet, within a very few years, it evaporated. England's slow homecoming from the war was as if Odysseus had come back to Ithaca at last, only to find that Penelope had married one of her suitors and to hear news from afar that Troy had rebuilt itself from the ashes and was doing rather well. It is surely one of the great disappointments of world history. Of the other three major Allied countries that had won the war, the USA and Russia were hegemonic global powers and France was energized by its first thorough-going industrial revolution. Only Britain had to cope with the moral deflation of anti-climax.

During the war, one of the leading English intellectuals, Cyril Connolly, could write almost matter-of-factly of the post-war order that 'It will be a world in which the part played by the English will be of supreme importance... England will find itself in the position of one of those fairy-tale princes who drift into a tournament, defeat a dragon or wicked knight, and then are obliged to marry the king's daughter and take on the cares of a confused, impoverished, and reactionary kingdom. That kingdom is Europe...'[7] The implicit concern was that England would be marrying beneath it – that its advances might be rejected was unimaginable.

The fairy-tale English Kingdom of Europe did not come into being. James Morris gave voice to a heartfelt lament. Contrasting the psychological state of the nation in 1962, when its first effort to join the Common Market was about to be rebuffed, with that in the war years, he wrote that in just fifteen years, the 'feeling of happy supremacy' he had felt as a young cavalryman had vanished.

> So complex is the transition through which our people are presently passing, that frank pride of country has all but gone by the board, and patriotism is very nearly a dirty word. Only fifteen years, and today the intelligent young Englishman all too often seems trapped in a drab web of inferiority.

When collective moods swing so radically from pole to pole, it is a safe bet that what is happening is not a transition from one to the other but a constant hovering between them. Between psychological extremities, to adapt W. B. Yeats, England must run its course. The 'feeling of happy supremacy' co-exists with the sense of being trapped in a 'drab web of inferiority'. The power of Brexit is that it promised to end at last all this tantalizing uncertainty by fusing these contradictory moods into a single emotion – the pleasurable self-pity in which one can feel at once horribly hard done by and exceptionally grand. Its promise is, at heart, a liberation, not from Europe, but from the torment of an eternally unresolved conflict between superiority and inferiority.

It is striking, looking back on English intellectual opinion about the merits or demerits of joining the Common Market as expressed in the leading monthly journal of liberal intellectual debate, *Encounter*, to find these extremes of self-aggrandizement and self-abasement. On the one hand, there is the hubris.

Morris, in his reflections on the great change of mood, could still console himself with the obvious truth that England was morally and culturally superior: 'More than most Powers, we can still presume to precedence in teaching nations how to live'.[8] Even in making the argument in 1971 that Britain should stay out of Europe and forget all its pretensions to be a world power, Joan Robinson, professor of economics at the University of Cambridge, appealed to a notion of innate moral superiority that could be nurtured in splendid isolation: 'I think that, as empires go, the British Empire was not discreditable and that to give it up (in the main) without a fight was a very unusual example of common sense. Let us now have enough sense to accept the position of a small country and try to show the world how to preserve some elements of civilisation and decency that the large ones are rapidly stamping out.'[9]

Nancy Mitford, contemplating the prospect of Britain helping to build a new European empire asked (half-facetiously) 'What about Prince Charles as Emperor? The name is auspicious and the person very suitable.'[10] (The frustration of being still only poor Prince Charles almost fifty years after this was written must be deepened by the knowledge that he could have been Charlemagne.) The great violinist Yehudi Menuhin suggested (not at all facetiously) that Britain's ruling class, now that it was no longer running half the world, should offer itself for hire to lesser polities: 'I must confess to a bias. I have often thought, now that the days of Empire are changed, that Britain... with her great administrative experience and remarkable achievement in the Civil Service should offer a world-wide service called "Rent-a-Government" which would take its place among the enormous combines which build dams or cities, or provide insurance or advice on investment.' The White Man's Burden, stoically assumed in the imperial propaganda of F. D. Lugard and Rudyard Kipling, could now be turned into a nice little earner.

Menuhin also suggested that the hard-working Germans might wish to subsidize the leisure of the English. He wondered 'whether... German citizens will underwrite the perhaps less efficient British industries and their workers. Actually, the latter is not a bad idea, for it would enable the British worker to be the "test pilot" to explore on behalf of all mankind the use of leisure by the industrial populations at large.'[11]

(Such fantasies were not entirely confined to artists and intellectuals. At the start of the 1970s, a Gallup poll had suggested that 43 per cent of Britons expected that because of the wonders of new technology they would only have to work three days a week.[12] When the three-day week did arrive in December 1973 it was, alas, in rather grimmer circumstances.)

Less obviously ludicrous but no more fantastical was a notion that would return in full force with Brexit: that British superiority could be reborn in a new union, not with Europe, but with the old English-speaking and mainly white Empire. The historian Robert Conquest imagined in 1971 that this alternative superstate would keep the Europeans from going too far wrong:

The direction in which Britain should seek closer ties is within its own tradition of language, law, and politics; that is, with the United States, Canada, Australia, New Zealand, Ireland and the Caribbean Commonwealth countries... now that the United States has virtually admitted its inability to cope more or less alone with world problems, it too has a motive for a larger union of this sort. I would also argue that a United Europe without us would be stronger and safer under the protection of a much larger and more powerful 'Anglo-Saxon' union than if further increased in size and power itself, and so more liable to... dangerous delusions.[13]

This particular fantasy would return in Brexit: the idea that leaving the EU would allow Britain to take its more natural place in the reconstituted white empire of the 'Anglosphere'. One solution to the idea of being simultaneously small and great, underdog and overdog, has been, in Linda Colley's words, 'a persistent inclination to pursue empire vicariously by clambering like a mouse on the American eagle's head'.[14]

Even in the more realistic White Paper on entry to the Common Market, published in July 1971, a certain self-importance was taken for granted: 'The entry of the United Kingdom into the European Communities is... an issue of historic importance, not only for us, but Europe and the world.'[15] And, at a more demotic level, the idea of surrendering to necessity could be fused with a vivid self-regard – we may be having to join the continentals after all but by God they're lucky to have us. The very popular *Daily Express* columnist Jean Rook marked the moment of entry to the Common Market on New Year's Day 1973: 'Since Boadicea, we British have slammed our seas in the faces of invading frogs and wops, who start at Calais. Today, we're slipping our bolts. And, of all that we have to offer Europe, what finer than contact with our short-tongued, stiff-necked, straight-backed, brave, bloody-minded and absolutely beautiful selves? To know the British (it takes about 15 years to get on nodding terms) will be Europe's privilege.'[16]

Delusions, of themselves, are not necessarily neurotic. The trouble comes when you keep shifting between two opposing frames of mind. For side by side with this grandiosity there was a sense of abjection. A common theme in the early 1970s is that Britain is such a failure that it has no choice but to join the Europeans. The image is not that of a fabulous dynastic union but, rather, of a grumpy old bachelor settling for a bad marriage because the alternative is a slow death in miserable loneliness. The military historian Michael Howard writes in 1971, 'Nor is it clear that Western Europe will be made any richer, or happier, or more powerful if we do join. But the probability remains strong, that we will be poorer, more miserable and even more impotent than we are at present if we do not. The issue is no longer one that excites me very much.'[17] Donald Tyerman, former editor of *The Economist*, went so far as to suggest that Britain might not even be worthy of Common Market membership: 'As an observer, the biggest change since 1962–63 seems to me to be that, whereas then the sticking question was whether Europe was fit for us to join, the question now is, at bottom, whether we are fit to join Europe. If we go into that kitchen, can we stand the heat?'[18]

Joining was framed for the British, not as an act of collective will, but as a collective surrender of will. As the architect Sir Hugh Casson put it, using the advice rapists give to their victims: 'it's bound to happen anyway, so why not lie back and enjoy it?'[19] The sense is not so much that Britain wants to go into the Common Market, but that, in Marghanita Laski's plaintive question: 'Where else can we go?'[20] Britain had been evicted from its imperial palace and must either take the council's offer of a dull suburban house or become homeless in the world. As the 1971 White Paper put it: 'In a single generation we should have renounced an imperial past and rejected a European future. Our friends everywhere would be dismayed. They would rightly be as uncertain as ourselves about our future role and place in the world... Our power to influence the Communities would steadily diminish, while the Communities' power to affect our future would as steadily increase.'[21]

But there was between these co-existing alternatives of airy haughtiness and dejected resignation, a third possibility: fecklessness. It is shocking in retrospect to consider how many leading English intellectuals, caught between the conviction of superiority and the feeling of impotence, simply opted out. One of the modes of the privileged classes in England is a studied ennui, a pose of perfect indifference. In *Encounter*'s symposiums on whether or not to join Europe in 1962 and 1971, there is a significant strain of lazy world-weariness. Casson tartly expressed his 'disregard for those intellectuals who... either, protested, often at some length, their inability to understand the implications – what are intellectuals for? – or who, from the shelter of a comfortably cushioned chair, said the matter was of little interest since for them life will go on just as before'.

He was not wrong. Perhaps the best-known English historian of the time was the original 'TV don' A. J. P. Taylor, a conscious

'Little Englander'. Here he is on the Common Market: 'There is no British opinion about "going into Europe" intellectual or otherwise. No one understands it. No one cares about it, for or against, except perhaps for a few politicians who have taken up the affair as a means of professional advancement. Maybe it is the most decisive moment in British history since the Norman conquest or the loss of America. No one takes any notice all the same... Entry into Europe is the greatest non-question of all time.'[22] This was not in fact true of the general public: when, a month after Taylor wrote this, the government's White Paper on entry went on sale, there were queues outside the bookshops. It sold over a million copies, making it the best-selling official document in British history. During that month of July 1971, 100,000 people a week paid their 25 pence for a copy.

The boredom was, rather, a projection of intellectual irres-ponsibility that amounted to a treason of the clerks. John Sparrow, Warden of All Souls College, Oxford, and author, ironically, of *Controversial Essays*, was not untypical: 'Flattered as I am to be asked to contribute to your symposium about "Going into Europe", I am afraid I cannot supply you with a useful answer. This is a topic about which I am both ignorant and undecided. I don't know which side I ought to be on and I don't even know which side I *am* on.' The novelist John Braine wrote, 'If I were an editor, nothing would induce me to publish even one short article about the Common Market, let alone a symposium. The subject bores me stiff.'[23] Kenneth Clarke, who interpreted civilization for the masses in his Olympian TV programmes, replied to *Encounter*'s invitation with a terse dismissal: 'Like E. M. Forster, "I cannot make out", so am not qualified to make any statement at all. (Instincts all against.)'[24]

So, besides grandiosity and gloom, there was always intellectual indolence. It is important to keep this in mind because it is a strain in English public discourse about Europe that would never go away. It was in part a tic of the class system: it doesn't do for a fellow to seem to care very much about anything. In the early period of Britain's engagement with the European project, it took the form of an exaggerated boredom. But it was easy to convert affected boredom into mock-hysteria, easy to turn patrician languor into a sense that the whole thing is a jolly game. Each is a way of saying that none of it really matters, and of brushing off any real responsibility for the consequences. The form of irresponsibility would change, but the fundamental attitude would remain, especially among the occupants of comfortably cushioned chairs for whom 'life will go on just as before' whether or not Britain is in the EU. The droll affectation would prove to be a deadly affliction.

At the point of entry in 1973, however, the two main ingredients of pleasurable self-pity – a sense of one's own superiority and a feeling that one is unjustly beaten down – still existed separately. They had not yet been combined in the toxic cocktail that the Brexiteers would convince a majority of their compatriots to swallow in 2016. For that to happen, three conditions would have to be fulfilled. The first was a renewed sense of disappointment; the second a shift in the nature of the British scapegoat; the third the undermining of the great British compensation for its loss of global prestige.

Given the rather tepid 'where else would we go?' argument in favour of joining the Common Market, it is not surprising that it was never a popular cause. As late as April 1970, polls showed that a mere 19 per cent favoured entry, while 57 per cent thought Britain's application should be dropped altogether even before the talks on it were due to begin in June. Nor was there anything like a political consensus. Labour was largely sceptical and the thirty-seven Tory MPs who voted against entry in October 1971 made up the largest backbench Conservative rebellion since the vote of no confidence in Neville Chamberlain in 1940. Membership of the Common Market was therefore sold – and grudgingly accepted – primarily as a sovereign remedy for Britain's economic ills.

But the expectation that entry would allow Britain to transcend the disappointed expectations of the post-war years was itself disappointed. First impressions last – it matters that the decade after the UK joined was in fact 'the most dreadful of the postwar era, a litany of racial conflict in England, nationalist discontent in Scotland and Wales, war in Ireland and perpetual strikes everywhere'.[25] Instead of the turbo-charged lift-off into the future, the British Seventies were, according to Francis Wheen: 'one long Sunday evening, heavy with gloom and torpor'[26] though it was surely a particularly manic kind of torpor.

The years in which Britain decided to join and then settled into membership of the Common Market were notably panicky. As Wheen has pointed out, 'In the twenty years between 1950 and 1970... a state of emergency had been declared only twice, for the national rail strike of 1955 and the seamen's strike of 1966. During Ted Heath's brief and calamitous premiership, between June 1970 and February 1974, he declared no fewer than five.'[27] Thus, on either side of the momentous decision to join the European project, Britain was in crisis mode. These five national emergencies may have planted the seeds of one of the tropes that would surface in the coming decades and flower in Brexit: the idea that Britain was, in some way, still at war.

This great disappointment led on to the second condition: the question of who is to blame? And here, there was a gradual and deeply ironic change. England in the 1960s and 1970s was flagrantly racist. There was a ready and visible target for those looking for someone to blame for the country's economic and social ills – black people, who had themselves replaced Jews in the role. (It is not coincidental that the last English anti-Semitic riots took place in 1947, just ten months before the arrival of the *Empire Windrush* carrying the first wave of post-war immigrants from the Caribbean.) Racism most certainly did not disappear in the 1980s and 1990s, but its open expression did become much more unacceptable in politics, public discourse and popular culture. After Enoch Powell destroyed his mainstream political career with the inflammatory racism of his 'rivers of blood' speech in April 1968, no senior figure with credible designs on power would again so explicitly blame blacks and Asians for England's failings. The dog whistle would replace the megaphone.

This left a vacancy, which was filled by the European Union. A particular irony is that the scapegoating of the EU as the eternal source of England's ills was facilitated in part by one of the more progressive developments in British culture: the gradual marginalization of open racism. 'Brussels,' as Richard Weight puts it, 'replaced Brixton as the whipping boy of British nationalists.'[28] That the EU did indeed partly occupy the space where open racism had once flourished is evident in the large overlap between pro-Brexit and anti-immigrant sentiment. But this suggests that much of the animosity was never really about the EU itself – it was a sublimated or displaced rage at Them. The black and brown Other fused with the European Other.

The third condition for the emergence of a politically potent self-pity was negative. In 1962, Arnold Toynbee made a crucial point about the ways in which the English had historically avoided occasions for self-pity:

> In the past the English have avoided the awful mistake of crying over spilt milk. They have quickly found and milked new cows, instead of standing still and wringing their hands.... In our day we have had recourse to this simple but effective British philosophy once again in meeting our own generation's ordeal. Recognising, as we did in good time, that the days of colonial rule were numbered, we decided to make the liquidation of our 19th-century Empire into a festival instead of a funeral.... Simultaneously we found another new world to win within the coasts of our own island. In our generation we have won not only the Commonwealth but the Welfare State... The Welfare State and the Commonwealth are obviously two of those exhilarating enterprises that are England's traditional prescription for easing the painfulness of change.[29]

Toynbee's point about the Commonwealth is probably, in the long term, wrong – it may have eased the pain of withdrawing from Empire but it has never been an English exhilaration. Yet the idea of the welfare state as a dike against the floods of tears over spilt milk is crucial. The building of the welfare state was a tangible rebuke to temptations to wallow either in empty fantasies of supremacy or in the masochistic delights of impotence. For the vast majority of people in the United Kingdom (and for my Irish relatives who emigrated partly to join that new social order) it represented stunning progress. The creation of an institution like the National Health Service was a novel kind of conquest, a turning of British energy inwards to face the great enemies of squalor and disease. It was indeed a new world that was won, and one that made more positive difference to British lives than the grabbing of colonies had ever done.

Conversely, the gradual erosion of the welfare state after the election of Margaret Thatcher in 1979 was, among other things, an undermining of the seawalls that kept those oceans of self-pity at bay. A welfare state is about the future – it gives young people a sense that they have one and older people the confidence not to fear their own. It creates a positive trajectory – my kids' lives will be better than mine. But when the welfare state starts to slip away, it becomes part of the past. It is regarded nostalgically, as an aspect of a lost golden age. This shift in time is one of the key reasons why there could after the end of the Seventies be no future in England's dreaming. England began to be viewed in the rear-view mirror.

There was always, moreover, a link between the rise of reactionary and xenophobic nationalism in England and inadequacies in the functioning of the welfare state. Camilla Schofield, in her reading of the tsunami of letters sent by supporters to Enoch Powell after the 'rivers of blood' speech predicting a racial apocalypse, notes that 'Powell's letter-writers speak of student protests, labour unrest, but most of all they speak of the indignities of declining welfare provisions – filled hospital beds and unavailable council houses... concern that immigration could destroy the National Health Service and public housing ran throughout.'[30] The Leave campaign in the Brexit referendum would of course make the same false connection: we are anti-immigrant because we wish to defend the welfare state. Powell didn't actually believe in the welfare state, and most of the leading Brexiteers don't either, but they knew that many of their supporters did so.

It may be, too, that what lingered in England's collective consciousness from the extraordinary success of the Labour government in creating the welfare state in a few short years after the end of the war was a distorted idea of radical change. What Britain experienced in those post-war years was a bloodless revolution – a rapid and radical reordering of society achieved democratically and without violence.

Brexit, too, is an attempt at a bloodless revolution and as such a kind of parodic replay of the previous one in which seriousness becomes game-playing, meticulous planning becomes seat-of-the-pants opportunism, a profound sense of public duty becomes narcissistic posturing and deep, difficult change becomes epic symbolism: the first time as policy, the second time as performance.

These three conditions – the renewal of disappointed expectations, the need for a new scapegoat and the erosion of the welfare state – allowed something quite extraordinary to happen. If England's deep problems were that it had lost an empire but not gained a role, and that it had won a great war but not gained the fruits of victory, a kind of solution became imaginatively possible: that the country should change places. This is one possible answer to the deflationary sensation so perfectly captured in a question mark in Jane Gardam's novel of the dissolution of the Raj, *Old Filth*: 'When empires end, there's often a dazzling finale – then—?'[31] Well, perhaps empires don't quite end when you think they do. Perhaps they have a final moment of zombie existence. This may be the last stage of imperialism – having appropriated everything else from its colonies, the dead empire appropriates the pain of those it has oppressed.

Instead of being an imperial power, could England not be imagined as a colony? Instead of being a victor, could England not be imagined as a defeated nation? These are crazy questions but the answer, it turned out in both cases, is yes. It is possible, when overlordship and victory turn sour, to think of oneself as the underdog and the loser. This would be, in Leigh Hunt's terms, the tribute that self-pity would pay to self-love, a masochistic desire to seek out humiliation combined with a grandiose sense that such humiliation was an outrage against an exceptionally fine people. And, as so often in history, what began as an imaginary indulgence would ultimately try to make itself a reality.

It does not seem entirely beside the point that, in the years immediately leading up to Brexit, by far the biggest-selling book by an English author in any genre was E. L. James's *Fifty*

Shades of Grey. It is a fantasy of submission and dominance. It is not hard to fantasize, in turn, a political adaptation in which Christian Grey is the European Union and Anastasia Steele an innocent England seduced into entering his Red Room of Pain.

For most of the readers of *Fifty Shades*, the appeal was entirely vicarious. It was not about anything that was or might be real in their lives. It was make-believe bondage – exactly like the Brexiteers' make-believe version of England's bondage to Europe. Grey is a Brexiteers' mad mirage of a Brussels bureaucrat. The book is not about sex – it is about rules. *Fifty Shades* is, indeed, hilariously bureaucratic. Submission, as it happens, is like EU membership: tediously legalistic. Poor Anastasia finds herself embroiled in complex negotiations before she can get down to business. It is not enough for the Europeans that they get to whip you – they have to torture you with paperwork as well:

> 'Here I was foolishly thinking that I'd spend a night of unparalleled passion in this man's bed, and we're negotiating this weird arrangement.'
> 'You mentioned paperwork.'
> 'Yes.'
> 'What paperwork?'

The novel comes complete with its own legal apparatus, its sado-masochistic treaty of accession: 'The Dominant and Submissive enter into this contract on the Commencement Date fully aware of its nature and undertake to abide by its conditions without exception.' Clause 15, paragraph 13 is the secret clause of the

European treaties that the Brexiteers always knew was there but could never read before: '15.13 The Submissive accepts the Dominant as her master, with the understanding that she is now the property of the Dominant, to be dealt with as the Dominant pleases during the Term generally but specifically during the Allotted Times and any additional agreed allotted times.'

James helpfully reminds her readers of the dictionary definition of submissive. In keeping with the great traditions of the epistolary novel, she reproduces an email:

> From: Christian Grey
> Subject: Your Issues
> Date: May 24 2011 01:27
> To: Anastasia Steele
>
> Dear Miss Steele,
> Following my more thorough examination of your issues, may I bring to your attention the definition of submissive.
> submissive [suhb-mis-iv] – adjective
> 1. inclined or ready to submit; unresistingly or humbly obedient [...]
>
> Synonyms: 1. tractable, compliant, pliant, amenable. 2. passive, resigned, patient, docile, tame, subdued. Antonyms: 1. rebellious, disobedient.
>
> Please bear this in mind for our meeting on Wednesday.

Anastasia, like much of the English population, is deeply uncertain. Rationally, she is drawn to political deal-making: 'What am I going to do? I want him, but on his terms? I just don't know. Perhaps I should negotiate what I want. Go through that ridiculous contract line by line and say what is acceptable and what isn't.' But, also like England in the sadomasochistic hallucinations of the Brexiteers, she cannot resist the 'sweet, agonizing torture' of playing Submissive to Brussels's Dominant. 'It is,' she concedes, 'so erotic. Truly I am a marionette and he is the master puppeteer.'

The political erotics of imaginary domination and imaginary submission are the deep pulse of the Brexit psychodrama. Wherein lies the vicarious thrill of imagining a wealthy, relatively successful twenty-first-century European country as a marionette controlled by a continental puppeteer? What kick can a still quite influential, prosperous, largely functional country get from thinking of itself, as foreign secretary Jeremy Hunt would do in October 2018, as a nation incarcerated in a neo-Stalinist prison of cruel subjection?

The frisson comes, surely, from the allure of irresponsibility. In the bondage games playing out in the English reactionary imagination, Britain has spent forty-five years hanging from the ceiling in the Red Room of Pain, with clamps on its nipples and a gag in its mouth. For a significant part of its ruling class, this is a posture of absolute powerlessness that corrupts absolutely. The deep problems of class and geographic division, increasing social squalor and rising inequality, cannot be its fault. It has an excuse for everything and responsibility for nothing. There is, paradoxically, a heady, reckless freedom in this dream of surrender. Willed helplessness becomes quite sexy. 'Picture yourself,' says Grey, 'lying here bound and totally at my mercy.' 'Oh my,' says Anastasia.

2.

SS-GB: LIFE IN OCCUPIED ENGLAND

[The idea of the nation] enables us to daydream as
we live out our lives, as the factory-girl daydreams
with the aid of her paperback thriller

—ENOCH POWELL

B efore the narrative of Len Deighton's best-selling thriller
SS-GB begins, there is a 'reproduction' of an authentic-
looking rubber-stamped document: 'Instrument of Surrender – English Text. Of all British armed forces in United
Kingdom of Great Britain and Northern Ireland including all
islands.' It is dated 18 February 1941. After ordering the cessa-
tion of all hostilities by British forces, it sets down further
conditions, including 'The British Command to carry out at
once, without argument or comment, all further orders that
will be issued by the German Command on any subject.
Disobedience of orders, or failure to comply with them, will

be regarded as a breach of these surrender terms and will be dealt with by the German Command in accordance with the laws and usages of war.' The novel was published in 1978. In 2014, the BBC announced plans for a five-part TV version, which was screened in 2017, shortly after the Brexit vote.

In the opening pages of the novel, set later in 1941, we meet Detective Superintendent Douglas Archer and his junior side-kick, Detective Sergeant Harry Woods. They have different attitudes to Britain's defeat and the German occupation: 'For Harry the fighting would never end. His generation, who'd fought and won in the filth of Flanders, would never come to terms with defeat. But Douglas Archer had not been a soldier. As long as the Germans let him get on with the job of catching murderers, he'd do his work as he'd always done it. He wished he could get Harry to see it his way.'[1]

Archer continues to work at 'Whitehall 1212, Headquarters of Kriminalpolizei, Ordnungspolizei, Sicherheitsdienst and Gestapo', reporting to Gruppenführer Fritz Kellermann. He is featured in a glossy propaganda magazine: 'Like most of London's policemen he welcomes the modern and scientific crime-fighting methods introduced by his new German com-mander. Superintendent Archer – and his colleagues – speak warmly of their General, and secretly refer to him as "Father".'

Winston Churchill has been executed by an SS firing squad. (It goes without saying that he refused a blindfold and flashed a V sign at his executioners.) The king, half dead from a bomb blast, is being held in the Tower of London. There are 'special Wehrmacht shows at the Palladium' and a 'notorious concentration camp at Wenlock Edge'. There is already 'a new class of men who had emerged from the wreckage of defeat': 'Members of Parliament and members of the puppet government who had learned to play their role in the new Nazi super-state that covered most of Europe... the men of Whitehall; top-ranking bureaucrats whose departments continued to run as smoothly under the German flag as they had under conservative and socialist governments.'

The Germans like Archer: 'He was "Germanic", a perfect example of "the new European".' And Archer in turn is sympathetic to Harry's difficulty in accommodating himself to these new realities: '"Age is an important part of it," said Douglas. "At Harry's age it's not easy to go suddenly from being at the heart of Empire to being an outpost of an occupied colony."'

Written amid the anxieties of Britain's early membership of the European Communities, Deighton's thriller sets up two ideas that will become important in the rhetoric of Brexit. Since there is no sense that Deighton has a conscious anti-EU agenda in any of this, these ideas seem to arise from a deeper structure of feeling in England. One is the fear of the Englishman like Archer turning into the 'new European', fitting himself into the structures of German domination. Archer, at least as we originally encounter him, is a harbinger of the 'rootless cosmopolitan' who cannot be trusted to uphold English independence and English values and who therefore functions as the enemy within, the quisling class of pro-Europeans. This is the treason of the elite, the puppet politicians and sleek mandarins who quickly accommodate themselves to the new regime. Deighton was building on real historical memories of the appeasers whose pre-war conduct makes the notion that they would have quickly become collaborators in the event of a defeat to the Nazis highly credible.

But this idea of a treacherous elite would later ferment into a heady and intoxicating brew of suspicion that the Brexiteers would both dispense to the masses and consume themselves.

The other crucial idea here is the vertiginous fall from 'heart of Empire' to 'occupied colony'. In the imperial imagination, there are only two states: dominant and submissive, colonizer and colonized. This dualism lingers. If England is not an imperial power, it must be the only other thing it can be: a colony. And, as Deighton successfully demonstrated, this logic can be founded in an alternative English history. The moment of greatest triumph – the defeat of the Nazis – can be reimagined as the moment of greatest humiliation – defeat by the Nazis. The pain of colonization and defeat can, in the context of uneasy membership of the EU, be imaginatively appropriated.

SS-GB was in part the inspiration for an even more successful English thriller, Robert Harris's multi-million-selling *Fatherland*, published in 1992 and filmed for television in 1994. Harris had begun the novel in the mid-1980s but abandoned it. He revived and finished it explicitly in the context of German reunification in 1990 and of fears that the enemy Britain had defeated twice in the twentieth century would end the century by dominating it: 'If,' Harris wrote in the introduction to the twentieth-anniversary edition in 2012, 'there was one factor that suddenly gave my fantasy of a united Germany a harder edge, it was the news that exactly such an entity was unexpectedly returning to the heart of Europe.'[2]

In retrospect, German reunification is perhaps the greatest missed opportunity for the English finally to have done with the war. Had there been a capacity to generate new narratives of Europe, this could have been shaped as a moment of British vindication – the final working-out of the consequences of Nazism. As Anthony Barnett puts it, 'The triumph and relief of the unification of Germany could and should have belonged to us in Britain, as well as to Germany itself. It was the final liberation from Nazism, the end of that country's punishment, a time to welcome a great culture back into our arms.'[3]

Why, then, were there no photographs of Margaret Thatcher and Helmut Kohl holding hands at the Brandenburg Gate to match the pictures of Kohl and François Mitterrand at Verdun in 1984? Because Thatcher literally carried in her handbag maps showing German expansion under the Nazis.[4] This was a mental cartography that English conservatism could not transcend – the map of a Europe that may no longer exist in reality but within which its imagination remains imprisoned. 'Europe,' Barnett writes, 'moved on from the Second World War and Britain didn't.' One might go so far as to say that England never got over winning the war.

In fact, Britain not only did not move on in 1990 – with the resurrection of a united Germany, it moved back. Harris is no anti-European reactionary and would in fact become one of the most furious critics of Brexit. Yet, like Deighton, he was tapping in to profound national anxieties. As a dark fantasy of British defeat, *Fatherland* is even bleaker than *SS-GB*.

It is set twenty years on from the British surrender – the protagonist remembers, in 1964:

Peace with the British in '44 – a triumph for the Führer's counter-intelligence genius! March remembered how all U-boats had been recalled to their bases on the Atlantic coast to be equipped with a new cipher system: the treacherous British, they were told, had been reading the Fatherland's codes. Picking off merchant shipping had been easy after that. England was starved into submission. Churchill and his gang of war-mongers had fled to Canada.[5]

While Deighton's novel is set immediately after a successful German invasion and deals in part with the emergence of a British Resistance, Harris leaves the reader with no such comfort. Churchill has not even had his final moment of glorious defiance: 'He's an old man now. In Canada. He lives there.'[6] So does Elizabeth, pretender to the British throne now reoccupied by her uncle King Edward VIII.

The German newspapers carry ads for 'French perfume, Italian silks, Scandinavian furs, Dutch cigars, Belgian coffee, Russian caviar, British televisions – the cornucopia of Empire spilled across the pages' – the Empire is now the Reich. There are snippets of news relating to Britain: 'Herbert von Karajan to conduct a special performance of Beethoven's Ninth Symphony – the European anthem – at the Royal Albert Hall in London on the Führer's birthday... In London it had been announced that King Edward and Queen Wallis were to pay a state visit to the Reich in July "further to strengthen the deep bonds of respect and affection between the peoples of Great Britain and the German Reich".'[7] But the real twist of the knife in Harris's story is that these are unimportant items of trivia concerning an unimportant satellite state of the Greater German Reich. The novel is set in Germany and the main characters are German. There is nothing of significance to say about England twenty years after its surrender.

Except, that is, that it is part of a European Union:

> In the West, twelve nations – Portugal, Spain, France, Ireland, Great Britain, Belgium, Holland, Italy, Denmark, Norway, Sweden and Finland – had been corralled by Germany, under the Treaty of Rome, into a European trading bloc. German was the official second language in all schools. People drove German cars, listened to German radios, watched German televisions, worked in German-owned factories, moaned about the behaviour of German tourists in German-dominated holiday resorts, while German teams won every international sporting competition except cricket, which only the English played.[8]

At one point, the hero, March, is walking in Berlin: 'He turned right at the European Parliament. The flags of the twelve member nations were lit by spots. The swastika which flew above them was twice the size of the other standards.'[9]

This mimics, of course, basic aspects of the actual European Community as it came to exist in 1992: the founding Treaty of Rome, the twelve members (with Norway and Finland filling in for Germany itself and Luxembourg which has been annexed to the Reich). But it specifically recasts the community as a forced creation of Germany that is dominated economically, linguistically and culturally by its Nazi masters.

The huge swastika flying above the flags of the twelve nations (including, by implication, the Union Jack) is a lurid image of the EU's reality as a German colonial project.

One need only fast-forward to a tweet in August 2018 by the former Tory and UKIP member of the European Parliament Roger Helmer to understand how literally this fantasy could be taken in Brexit discourse: 'When I was born, I was not a "European Citizen" (and my father's generation fought to ensure we should not be German citizens). I am determined that I shall not die as a European Citizen.'[10]

A dystopian fantasy this may be, but in the English reactionary imagination dystopian fantasy was and is indistinguishable from reality. Rhetorically, it was a commonplace among British anti-Europeans that the EU was a continuation in another, more insidious form, of previous attempts at domination from the continent. In 1989, for example, the Bruges Group of anti-European Tories heard Professor Kenneth Minogue of the London School of Economics tell them that 'the European institutions were attempting to create a European Union, in the tradition of the mediaeval popes, Charlemagne, Napoleon, the Kaiser and Adolf Hitler'.[11]

The sleight of hand was not subtle: Hitler tried to unite Europe, so does the EU, therefore the EU is a Hitlerian project. But the lack of subtlety did not stop the trope from being used in the Brexit campaign: 'Napoleon, Hitler, various people tried this [unifying Europe], and it ends tragically. The EU is an attempt to do this by different methods,' Boris Johnson told the *Daily Telegraph* on 15 May 2016, a month before the referendum. That Napoleon and 'various people' were not the point of the argument became clear in Johnson's reiteration of the real point: that the EU was 'pursuing a similar goal to Hitler in trying to create a powerful superstate'.

While Harris was writing *Fatherland* in 1990, the British secretary of state for trade and industry, Nicholas Ridley, a close friend and ally of the prime minister Margaret Thatcher, told the *Spectator* that the European Monetary System being introduced by the EU was 'all a German racket designed to take over the whole of Europe... I'm not against giving up sovereignty in principle, but not to this lot. You might as well give it to Adolf Hitler, frankly. ... I'm not sure I wouldn't rather have the shelters and the chance to fight back than simply being taken over by economics.'[12] The *Spectator*'s cover carried the headline 'Speaking for England' – a conscious reference back to one of the moments of high drama in September 1939 when Leo Amery in the House of Commons invited Labour's Arthur Greenwood to 'Speak for England!', implying that the appeasing prime minister Neville Chamberlain did not do so. Lest there be any doubt that Ridley was replaying the appeasement crisis, the cover cartoon showed him as having painted a Hitler fringe and moustache on the face of the then German chancellor Helmut Kohl.

Ridley's remarks were dismissed by Lutz Stavenhagen, minister of state in Kohl's administration, as the sort of thing that might be heard 'in the pub after a football match'.[13] And Ridley himself had to resign. But these were not the mere rantings of a marginal crank. As Peter Jenkins wrote in the *Independent* at the time, 'it is widely supposed that Mrs Thatcher's heart is with him, if not her head... It is no secret that she, like him, fears that monetary and economic union in Europe will become the tool of German domination rather than the means of containing a united Germany. She too instinctively mistrusts the Germans and finds it impossible to forget the experiences of the Second World War.'[14]

This was evidently true. In November 1974, when she was a contender for the leadership of the Conservatives, Thatcher confessed to the *Daily Express* that she was still indulging in the ultimate wartime pursuit: food hoarding. She revealed the contents of her emergency larder: eight pounds of granulated sugar, one pound of icing sugar, six jars of jam, six jars of marmalade, six jars of honey, six tins of salmon 'to make salmon mousse', four one-pound cans of corned beef, four one-pound cans of ham, two one-pound cans of tongue, one tin of mackerel, four tins of sardines; two one-pound jars of Bovril, twenty tins of various fruits, and 'one or two' tins of vegetables.[15] 'I resent,' she added, 'being called a hoarder.' Had she been able to see into the future, she might have pointed out that she was previewing her successors' plans for a possible no-deal Brexit.

On a more epic level, Thatcher had the Falklands War. It may have been a last hurrah for Britain's imperial pretensions, but it functioned even better as a kind of epilogue to the great psychodrama of the Second World War and a real-life version of the invasion thrillers. In her victory speech of July 1982, Thatcher was quite explicit in invoking the Falklands as a renaissance of the old wartime spirit, and victory as proof that Britain was no different then from what it had been during its Finest Hour. She chided those who believed that 'we could never again be what we were'. The doubters 'were wrong. The lesson of the Falklands is that Britain has not changed and that this nation still has those sterling qualities which shine through our history. This generation can match their fathers and grandfathers in ability, in courage, and in resolution. We have not changed. When the demands of war and the dangers to our own people call us to arms – then we British are as we have always been.'[16]

Yet even in this triumphal mode, Thatcher gave new life to the metaphors of retreat and invasion. 'We have ceased to be a nation in retreat,' she said, implying that the nation had been precisely that for a long time. 'Why,' she asked, 'do we have to be invaded before we throw aside our selfish aims and begin to work together...?'

Within this question is a claim: 'we' were invaded. The beauty of the Falklands conflict is that it played out the invasion fantasy of *SS-GB* – a fascist regime violating the sanctity of the homeland – but at a safe distance of almost 8,000 miles. The population of the Falklands – 1,820 people in 1982 – served as a metaphor for the UK. 'British people,' said Thatcher, 'had to be threatened by foreign soldiers and British territory invaded and then – why then – the response was incomparable.' Her plaintive question – 'Why do we have to be invaded before we throw aside our selfish aims and begin to work together?' – contained the assertion that 'we' were invaded by fascists: what had not happened in 1939–45 had finally happened in 1982.

It helped that the tiny Falklands population that was serving this microcosmic function was almost entirely white – a 'British people' that no longer existed – and that this 'British territory' was an almost entirely rural landscape. The Falklands was a kind of make-believe England with no black and brown immigrants. Its pre-industrial terrain was a fantasy version of the post-industrial landscape that Thatcher herself was in fact creating at home in England, without the empty steel plants and rusting machines. The Falklands was literally pastoral – home to 400,000 sheep and their shepherds – and a weird version of J. R. R. Tolkein's The Shire, itself in turn an imaginary rustic England threatened by power-mad fascistic invaders.

Thatcher's question, however, itself expressed a deeper fear. Even while celebrating the wartime spirit of Britain, she was asking why it could not express itself without war. While citing the Falklands as proof that Britain could 'again be what we were' in 1939–45, Thatcher was also raising an anxious query about Britain itself: was it only in wartime that it really existed as a polity that transcended its deep divisions of national identity and class interest? Without war, did it really exist at all? In retrospect, for a triumphal address, Thatcher's speech is remarkably open in its existential anxiety: 'British people had to be threatened by foreign soldiers and British territory invaded and then – why then – the response was incomparable. Yet why does it need a war to bring out our qualities and reassert our pride?'

Why do we have to be invaded in order to exist as a collective entity? It is a remarkable question for the leader of a state that had not in fact been successfully invaded since it was formed in 1707, and of an island that had not suffered any serious external invasion since 1066? Implied in the question is an existential terror: without invasion do 'we' really exist at all? In this light, novels like SS-GB and Fatherland are not just masochistic fantasies, they are symptoms of a much deeper pathology in which pain is an existential necessity. In this distorted self-image, the UK itself is like the body of Franken-stein's monster: it can be animated only by the galvanic shock of invasion. Without the collective anguish of forced penetration, it would have no underlying collective life at all. Thatcher's cry – 'All over Britain, men and women are asking – why can't we achieve in peace what we can do so well in war?' – is haunted by the most obvious answer: we can't. And as the subsequent failures of British military power in Iraq and Afghanistan would show, it was not just war that was needed to reassure Britain that it had a meaningful collective existence, it was the idea of invasion and submission.

The problem is that there was no sadist to act as the external partner required for this masochistic fantasy. The crypto-fascist Argentinian military junta served, for a short while, as the perfect collaborator, and the remarkable speed and power with which Britain responded to its aggression showed how deep a need it was fulfilling. But the fix was temporary. The Falklands was Britain as Fortinbras, who will 'find quarrel in a straw / When honour's at the stake'. It was not Britain as Hamlet, agonized by existential questions of purpose and meaning. And there was no one else to play the required role of invader – even the ramping up of the Soviet threat by Ronald Reagan and Thatcher was curiously ineffective, not least because the danger of nuclear war was too hugely existential to serve as a microcosmic metaphor.

The Falklands War, for all its grotesque elements, might have been a moment of release, a way of getting all the dark fantasies of invasion and heroic resistance out of England's system once and for all: this time we really were invaded by Nazis and we won. But Thatcher could not achieve this moment of release and transcendence because she could not answer her own question. The neoliberal project, with its flaying of the state, was entirely at odds with the collectivist command economy of wartime. Thatcher, in her victory speech, acknowledged that 'it took the battle in the South Atlantic for the shipyards to adapt ships way ahead of time; for dockyards to refit merchantmen and cruise liners, to fix helicopter platforms, to convert hospital ships'. In other words, without the South Atlantic, those dockyards would lie idle. In the wake of what was above all a demonstration of Britain's sea power, its shipyards would continue to close and dwindle. The great capacities of their workers would go back to being unwanted. A very different wartime metaphor would soon take hold: that Thatcher's governments did more damage to Britain's industrial cities than the Luftwaffe's bombing campaign.

There could be no release from the dark fantasies haunting the imagination of British conservatism, and there would continue to be a need for an imaginary invader and dominator. In 1990, while Germany was being reunified, there was very little depth to anti-German feeling in Britain – surveys at the time showed that most British people were in favour of German unity and trusted the Germans a lot or somewhat. The imagining of a German-dominated Europe through the evocation of Hitler was not an authentic popular prejudice against an old enemy. It was a way – albeit one that still seemed to have few real-world consequences – of thinking about the

European Union itself, of summoning it into being as the ghastly ghost, not just of the Nazis but of Nazis who had in reality won the war.

The war imagery filled a hole. England had no deep imaginative commitment to the European project. As an idea, the EU had a distinctly weak grip on English allegiance. It was always understood by most people as a more or less grudging concession to reality, a matter for resigned acceptance rather than joyous embrace. The popular mood a year after Britain joined was nicely captured by an official at the Department of Trade and Industry who likened the British public to 'a crowd of holidaymakers who, after much doubt and expense, have made a dangerous journey only to find the climate chilly, the hotel not what it was cracked up to be and the food too expensive… bloodthirsty feelings are mounting, not only towards the other nationalities in the hotel but to the courier who got them there.'[17]

The sheer volatility of public opinion in Britain was clear in the 1975 referendum on whether or not to stay in the Common Market: between January and June 1975, Harold Wilson's government managed to turn a 57 per cent Leave preference in polls to a 67 per cent Remain vote on the day.[18] The referendum was 'the only really sustained debate the British had ever had on their role in the world' and, as the *Daily Express* put it, in a jubilant editorial: 'Britain's Yes to Europe' had rung 'louder, clearer and more unanimous than any decision in peacetime history'.[19]

Yet a result that seemed both decisive and conclusive proved to be neither – Europe continued to poison British politics. And perhaps one of the reasons it did so is that, as the 1975 referendum campaign showed, there was a very deep under-lying division about the meaning of the Second World War. The war was – and remains – crucial in structuring English feel-ing about the European Union. In 1975, many of the leading advocates on both sides were veterans, as were many voters. But instead of this common experience creating a common emotional ideal of Britain's relationship to Europe, it fed two completely opposite stories, each very deeply felt.

One of these stories was that the catastrophic experience of the first half of the twentieth century carried two lessons that must never be forgotten: unrestrained nationalism led to war, and Britain could not stand aside from the fate of Europe. As Robert Saunders has shown, the successful pro-European campaigners in 1975 were both highly explicit and highly emotive in making these connections. For them, 'the emphasis was on the horror of war, which had devoured millions of lives in the prosecution of national rivalries. Britain in Europe used the poppy, the flower of remembrance, in its literature, while its logo was a dove of peace.' Pro-Europe posters said 'Nationalism kills' and 'No more Civil Wars'. Another, pub-lished for the anniversary of victory in Europe, directly evoked the joy of that triumph and sought to channel it into a sense that the Common Market *was* the great reward for victory: 'On VE Day we celebrated the beginnings of peace. Vote Yes to make sure we keep it.' Another poster read simply: 'Forty million people died in two European wars this century. Better lose a little sovereignty than a son or daughter.'[20]

These appeals worked for the majority of voters, but this very mention of sovereignty opened up, for a significant

minority, a gaping wound. 'For some,' writes Saunders, 'the surrender of national sovereignty to the EEC was a betrayal of all
those who had fought and died "to deliver Europe from Nazi
dictatorship".' A woman from Bournemouth wrote to the anti-
EEC Labour minister Barbara Castle that 'I... did not fight and
suffer a war for six years to be dictated to by the Germans.'
'Hitler's ghost,' wrote another of Castle's correspondents,
'must be shaking with laughter at Roy Jenkins, Hattersley &
the rest of the traitor crew.' Some, Saunders writes, 'viewed
the Community as a new power-grab by Germany, a country
which "on two occasions... has failed to conquer the British
militarily"'. For Castle's correspondents, the notion 'that the
GERMANS love us any more today than they did in 1914 &
1939' was dismissed with contempt. 'The leopard does not
easily change its spots.'

What's striking is that we can begin to see in this hysterical
rhetoric the outlines of two notions that would become crucial
to Brexit discourse. One is the comparison of pro-European
Brits to quislings, collaborators, appeasers and traitors. The
Leave campaign in 1975 likened the Treaty of Accession to the
Munich Agreement of 1938, remembered as a shameful act
of surrender to the Germans. Christopher Frere-Smith, who
ran the Get Britain Out campaign, warned repeatedly that
accession to the Common Market marked a 'new Munich',
with Ted Heath and Roy Jenkins (who was leading the In campaign) playing the roles of Neville Chamberlain and his foreign
secretary Lord Halifax. Voters were warned not be 'fooled by
the press bosses and the establishment politicians. They were
wrong about Hitler and they're wrong again.'

But the other idea is the fever-dream of an English Resistance, and its weird corollary: a desire to *have actually been invaded* so that one could – gloriously – resist. And not just resist but, in the ultimate apotheosis of masochism, die. Part of the allure of romantic anti-imperial nationalism is martyrdom. The executed leaders of the Easter Rising in Dublin in 1916, for example, stand as resonant examples of the potency of the myth of blood sacrifice. But in the ironic reversal of zombie imperialism, the appropriation of the imagery of resistance to a former colonizing power, this romance of martyrdom is mobilized as defiance of the EU.

In his anguished complaint about the vitiating effects of membership of the Common Market in 1977, Enoch Powell lamented: 'The breath which condemns submission to laws this nation has not made condemns submission to scales of value which this nation had not willed. To both sorts of submission I ascribe the haunting fear, which I am sure I am not alone in feeling, that we, the British, will soon have nothing left to die for. That was not a slip of the tongue. What a man lives for is what a man dies for, because every bit of living is a bit of dying. Patriotism is to have a nation to die for, and to be glad to die for it – all the days of one's life.'[21] This takes martyrdom to new levels of self-annihilating fantasy: death in the anti-EU resistance is not a fate or even an act. It is a daily pleasure.

The anti-Europe campaign in 1975 very consciously evoked the language of wartime resistance. The Common Market Safeguards Campaign published a newspaper called *Resistance News*, and the group of MPs around the leading Tory leaver,

Neil Marten, was known as the 'R' Group – R for resistance. During the war, Marten had been dropped into both France and Norway to work with the resistance movements, so presumably his followers could think of themselves operating behind enemy lines in deepest Dorset. All of this is much more *'Allo, 'Allo!* than *Army of Shadows*, tragedy played out the second time as farce. But, in what would become the camp sitcom of Brexit, that would not diminish its force.

It is worth noting in passing that this auto-cruelty was not unprecedented – a version of it existed even during the actual war. In this version, what was at work was not so much the desire to be invaded as the idea that parts of England somehow *deserved* to be bombed by the Luftwaffe. Cyril Connolly wrote in *Horizon* in 1943:

There are vast districts of London – Bayswater, for example, or Kensington – which seem to have been created for destruction, where squares and terraces for half a century have invited dilapidation, where fear and hypocrisy have accumulated through interminable Sunday afternoons until one feels, so evil is the atmosphere of unreality and suspense, that had it not been for the bombers, the houses would have been ignited one day of their own accord by spontaneous combustion. Behind the stucco porches and the lace curtains the half-life of decaying Victorian families guttered like marsh-gas. One has no pity for the fate of such houses, and no pity for the spectacular cinemas and fun-palaces of Leicester Square, whose architecture was a standing appeal to heaven to rain down vengeance on them.[22]

John Betjeman had already summoned the Heinkel HE 111s in 1937: 'Come friendly bombs and fall on Slough! / It isn't fit for humans now...' There was in the English imagination, long before *Fatherland* in the 1990s, already this strain of demented death-wishing, an ecstatic acid trip in which snobbish disgust at actual English modernity – cinemas, fun-palaces, suburbs – tips over into a lust for self-destruction. A fallen England deserves the punishment of bombardment or invasion, a purgatorial vengeance that will shock it back to itself. A good thumping would get the true blood flowing again. The problem with the EU, in this disordered mindset, is not that it is an invading force but that its takeover is too stealthy to deliver the salutary shock of deserved punishment.

Europe's role in this weird psychodrama is entirely pre-scripted. It does not greatly matter what the European Union is or what it is doing – its function in the plot is to be a more insidious form of Nazism. This is important to grasp, because one of the key arguments in mainstream pro-Brexit political and journalistic discourse would be that Britain *had* to leave because the Europe it had joined was not the Europe it found itself part of in 2016. In Andrew Gilligan's formulation on the fortieth anniversary of British accession in 2012, 'The British people joined, and were happy to join, a common market. They did not sign up to a social chapter, a single currency or any moves down the road to a superstate.'[23] Or as Boris Johnson put it in September 2017, the 'post-imperial future' was 'sold to the people purely as a common market, a way of maximising trade'. But 'Then came the gradual realisation that this was a very different agenda, an attempt not just at economic but political integration of a kind that the British people had never bargained for.'[24]

In itself, this is no more than usually mendacious – the truth being that 'ever closer union' was always an explicit part of what the British signed up to in 1973 and voted for in 1975. What matters, though, is the *way* it misses the point. The *idea* of Europe as a soft-Nazi superstate was vividly present in 1975, even when the still-emerging EU had a much weaker, less evolved and less intrusive form. The imaginary existential struggle between the gallant English Resistance and the Euro-reich was already being played out in one part of English consciousness. It was not a product of the ways in which the nine-member Common Market became the twenty-eight-member European Union. It was a product of England's deeply divided and strangely unsettled relationship to the Second World War and what it meant.

This is why it did not disappear after the apparently conclusive decision of 1975. It lay quiet for a while but emerged again in an appropriately demented form – the mad cow war. This half-forgotten episode of national hysteria is notable in the first place because the crisis that led to it was entirely self-inflicted by the British state. And it was, furthermore, an example, not of the alleged overregulation of British life by Brussels but of reckless underregulation driven by neoliberal 'free market' ideology. Yet it came to be construed as a replay of the Second World War, a lurid example of the interaction between shame, scapegoating and self-pity.

The mad cow crisis had its roots in 1981, when Margaret Thatcher's government was in the full flush of its early zeal.

Proposals for tight controls over the processing of animal protein that had been prepared under the previous Labour government were dropped, and instead ministers decided the industry itself should decide how best to manufacture meat and bone meal that was fed to cattle.[25] The industry lowered the temperatures at which rendering of sheep offal was carried out. As a result, sheep scrapie was passed on to cattle in the form of BSE, which then further spread as the parts of diseased cows were themselves converted to animal feed. This entered the food chain and created a human form of the disease, Creutzfeldt-Jakob Disease (CJD), which inflicted a slow and agonizing death on its victims.

The official response to this potential disaster was summed up in a staged event in May 1990, the same month in which the two German states signed a treaty of reunification. The Tory agriculture minister John Gummer force-fed his own four-year-old daughter Cordelia a beef burger in front of TV camera crews and newspaper reporters. This was a genuine moment of national humiliation, the ideas both of good government and of 'the roast beef of Old England' as a symbol of national identity turned to grotesque self-mockery. Someone had to be to blame – and it was, of course, the Germans. Germany, frustrated at the very slow and weak response of the European Union, imposed a unilateral ban on the import of British beef. This became a declaration of war, with England again standing alone against the Teutonic menace.

'Germans urged to call truce in "mad cow" war' ran the *Daily Mail* headline in January 1990 over a report that claimed Britain's chief veterinary officer Keith Meldrum had staged a 'confrontation' in Brussels and demanded that the Germans 'prove that British beef is unsafe'. While the Germans were asking for beef imports to be accompanied by certificates that they were free of BSE, Meldrum said, 'I will not issue those totally and completely unnecessary certificates. British meat is absolutely healthy. I've not changed my eating habits.' The subtext in the report was that it was a declaration of hostilities by the Germans to refuse to take an Englishman's word: 'West Germany was under pressure yesterday to end its "mad cow" war which is costing British farmers millions of pounds in lost beef exports.'[26]

This German 'war' lasted in the right-wing English press for a full decade – almost twice as long as the actual war of which it was a hallucinatory reprise. The War of Cordelia's Burger was fought mostly through journalistic hyperventilation. 'A small Somerset town finds itself at war with Germany' is the headline on a 1996 report in the *Daily Express* that representatives from the Bavarian town of Immenstadt had asked not to be served British beef at a ceremony in Wellington to mark the twinning of the two towns.[27] 'Kohl's beef blitzkrieg' (*Express*, 9 May 1996), 'French set to back down as Germans hot up beef war' (*Express*, 1 November 1999), 'Beef War: I'll Bring Britain To Its Knees' (*Express*, 27 October 1999), 'Battle lines drawn for new beef war' (*Daily Mail*, 5 August 1999), 'Time to retaliate' (*Daily Mail* editorial, 9 October 1999 – 'The British government should order immediate retaliatory action') – the war dragged ever onwards. The *Daily Express* even managed to place it deep within England's military history, with a photograph, under the banner 'Stop the Euro-Rot' and the headline 'Beefeaters sign on for a steak in history', of three newly recruited Tower of London guards in their faux-medieval uniforms: 'Britain signed up three new recruits yesterday as the battle raged to save our beef from the bureaucrats of Brussels. And with centuries of proud tradition behind them, Beefeaters Andrew Thomson, Trevor Hughes and Philip Parker swore allegiance to the Queen and their favourite meat.'[28] The men looked sternly ready to force-feed German children with honest British burgers.

In 1996, when England hosted the European Football Championship, one Tory minister, Gillian Shepherd, objected to the use of Beethoven's 'Ode to Joy' as the official anthem of the championship because the composer was German. Under the headline 'The Dunkirk spirit', *The Times* reported that the German team at Euro '96 was importing its own beef: 'the Football Association was displaying a healthy Dunkirk spirt. Scotch beef is still on the menu for England.'[29] The *Sun* warned its readers of 'a showdown' with the European Community 'on a scale rarely seen since the Battle of Britain'. The beef ban was forcing 'us to fight to save our traditions and freedoms'. The paper urged its readers to harass German tourists – and even to boycott German pornographic films.[30] The *Daily Mail* offered readers a handy list of items they could boycott in order to do their part in the war: 'Cut out and take when you go shopping: Say NO to these German... foods', including Tesco Black Forest Ham, Black Tower wine, Milka chocolate and John West canned herring fillets.[31]

Ludicrous as all of this is, it should be borne in mind that the tabloids had no trouble finding scholarly intellectuals to justify it. In a double-page spread in 1999, the *Daily Mail* ran a large photo of fake Nazis from *'Allo 'Allo!* with a think-piece headlined 'In the week that Germany kept the old feud alive by illegally banning British beef: Why it's a good thing for us to be beastly to the Germans.' It was written, not by some hack, but by the distinguished historian Niall Ferguson. He found a way to argue both that the 'war' with Germany was entirely phoney and that it was nonetheless worth continuing because it was somehow in Europe's best interests. While conceding 'The reality is that we have more in common with the Germans than with any other European people', Ferguson managed to conclude that '*bad* Anglo-German relations were (paradoxically) a good thing. To be precise: it would really be rather bad for everyone else in Europe if Britain and Germany did strike up a firm alliance.'[32]

This, too, is highly characteristic of the kind of discourse from which Brexit emerged, a peculiar cocktail of raw xenophobic hysteria, cool intellectual glibness and pure pantomime. The invasion metaphor could be deployed slickly by a high-class columnist like Michael Gove in *The Times*: 'The Social Chapter opt-out has been a legislative Maginot Line, unable to prevent directives infiltrating British law.'[33] Or it could be full, foaming self-lacerating rage at the native quislings kowtowing to the Euronazis, as in a *Mail* article by Simon Heffer: 'It is typical of this gutless Government, in its prostrate dealings with our masters in Brussels, that it should represent the avoidance of a complete humiliation by trumpeting a partial one as some sort of triumph.'[34]

Yet what brings these disparate modes together is the lure

of self-pity, the weird need to dream England into a state of awful oppression. If we return to Nicholas Ridley's rant, the striking thing is the way it wishes Britain back into wartime: 'I'd rather have the shelters and the chance to fight back.' This suggests that what Britain was experiencing in the 1990s at the hands of the EU was actually worse than the war of 1939–45 in which it triumphed.

And what could be worse than winning the war? Only losing it. Ridley's conjuring of the EU as a 'German racket designed to take over the whole of Europe' evokes a worse kind of invasion than that in Deighton's *SS-GB*: invasion by stealth. The suggestion is that a physical invasion by the Nazis would have been preferable to the membership of the EU which achieved the same ends by more cunning and dishonourable means.

At least the Nazis could have been, in Churchill's great and galvanic rhetoric, fought on the beaches, hills, fields and streets. They offered the 'chance to fight back'. The new German invasion, cloaked in the guise of peaceful co-operation, is more damnable because it does not give the English Resistance a proper physical target. Hostility to the EU thus opens the way to a bizarre logic in which a Nazi invasion would have been, relatively speaking, welcome. And of course this twisted reasoning is also self-generating: the very nonexistence of the invasion, the lack of any evidence beyond the German reluctance to emulate Cordelia Gummer and submit to being fed BSE burgers is an enraging proof of its insidiousness.

This is a deeply strange kind of displacement – a victor learning to think like the vanquished. But it makes a kind of sense. On the one hand, as the White Paper on entry to the Common Market emphasized in 1971, the experience of *not* being invaded was one of the genuinely distinctive things about being British: 'Our physical assets and our economy had suffered less disastrously than those of other Western European countries as a result of the war: nor did we suffer the shock of invasion. We were thus less immediately conscious of the need for us to become part of the unity in Europe...'[35] Yet the paper went on to contrast the fate of Britain since the war with that of the six members of the existing Common Market, all of whom *had* been invaded:

> The contrast between their experiences in recent years as members of the Communities, and ours outside, when our resources have not been growing sufficiently to do all we should like to do at home and abroad, suggests that they chose the right road... All the Community countries enjoyed rates of growth of gross national product (GNP) per head of population, or of private consumption per head, roughly twice as great as Britain's...[36]

It was not entirely ridiculous at some subliminal level to see these two things – being invaded and growing twice as fast as the country that wasn't – as cause and effect. The 'right road' to prosperity did not seem to lie through successful self-defence – on the contrary, invasion worked well for the Six. Britain was genuinely in a topsy-turvy situation, the winner that had been surpassed by the losers. Why not draw a topsy-turvy conclusion: in a dark stratum of the reactionary mind, we must think of ourselves as a defeated nation? And if Britain was to be defeated, the EU must be its invasive oppressor. Must be because there was no other possible candidate.

The very absurdity of this notion was its strength. The paranoiac must at some stage ask himself: but *why* are they out to get me? Since there was no actual evidence of any Western European hostility, the answer must lie in some deeply hidden motivation. How could they hate us when we saved them in the war? The proto-Brexiteers came up with a counter-factual truth that was at the same time highly satisfying: they hate us *because* we saved them.

Bernard Connolly, an English economist sacked by the European Commission because he had objected (not unreasonably) to the creation of the euro currency and an influential figure in subsequent anti-EU discourse in England, explained the mystery in 1996 specifically in the context of the BSE war: '"Britain Screwed by Europe" has been the recurrent experience ever since Edward Heath took us into the then EEC. Why? Is it just that our government and civil servants have been a soft touch?' No, he suggested, this was not enough to explain the malice because

> our Continental 'partners' should love us. But they do not. Do they despise us for our weakness? Or is there something about the way we think and do things that just gets up Continental noses? Are we being punished for being British? There is certainly a feeling in Europe that Britain has got away too lightly in the bloody mess that Europe has been since history began. In particular we are the one EU nation (with the exception of Sweden...) that escaped

catastrophic military defeat, occupation, dictatorship, or dismemberment in or after the Second World War. All that is regarded as 'not fair' by the politicians and bureaucrats of our Continental neighbours. To make things even worse, it was British resistance to Hitler that kept the spark of freedom and civilisation alive until the European war became a world war. The decadence of the French ruling class contributed disgracefully to France's military defeat. And that class and its successors has never forgiven the Western allies for inflicting the even greater humiliation of rescuing their country.[37]

This is the perfect-circle of self-pity and self-love: we deserve to be loved but we are hated because we are so wonderful.

Len Deighton's imaginary surrender order had deep roots in British public debate. Since the English mood in relation to joining Europe was largely one of surrendering to necessity, it was not so hard to think of the act as surrender full stop. In *Encounter*'s 1971 symposium on whether the UK should join the Common Market, for example, Sir William Hayter, Warden of New College, Oxford, and former British Ambassador to Moscow, looked back on his contribution to its debates almost a decade earlier: 'in 1962 I wrote that "in a few years we shall have to make an unconditional surrender to get in." I am afraid those few years have gone by, and now it is not even certain that an unconditional surrender will get us in.'[38]

Peter Shore MP, the most persistent Labour Party critic of Europe, during the 1975 referendum took up this theme: 'What the advocates of membership are saying... is that we are finished as a country; that the long and famous story of the British nation and people has ended; that we are now so weak and powerless that we must accept terms and conditions, penalties and limitations almost as though we had suffered defeat in a war.'[39] *As though we had suffered defeat in a war* – there is no phrase more accurately expressive of the extraordinary embrace by the victors of the self-pity of the vanquished.

These images would return in the immediate years before Brexit. In Owen Sheers' novel *Resistance*, published in 2007 and adapted for film in 2011, it is the autumn of 1944: 'First the failed landings in Normandy. Then the German counter-attack. The pages of the newspapers were dark with the print of the casualty lists. London was swollen with people fleeing north from the coast...'[40] The theme of quislings and traitors is taken up: it turns out that the Allied D-Day invasion plans had been betrayed to the Germans by a sleeper agent posing as 'a bank clerk in Brighton'. As the Germans advance into England, there are 'calls for peace, for surrender, from politicians the Home Service called "traitors"'. Native collaborators are operating ahead of the German advance, spreading rumours and panic. When one is caught, 'His accent had been perfect but then it transpired this wasn't because he was German at all but English.' A German proclamation says that 'British authorities may continue to function if they maintain a correct attitude'. The comic old codgers of Dad's Army are being ruthlessly slaughtered by the Wehrmacht: 'The British soldier was old... Grey hair, rheumy eye. Ehrhardt had bayoneted him with anger, with force, in textbook style. And now here he was laughing.' Nelson's Column is 'sliced in two and tipped onto the loading platforms of a transport lorry to be taken back as a trophy to Berlin'. Hitler stands on Parliament Hill 'promising "to bring peace at last to this nation misguided for so long by the corrupt democracy that once sat in those shattered buildings beneath us"'.[41] Churchill has followed King George to Canada. Rab Butler heads a quisling government based in Harrogate. An SS Albion division is formed.

Strikingly, when men of fighting age are deported, 'The German propaganda machine and William Joyce's BBC were calling these deportations Britain's contribution to "the rebuilding of a new United Europe".' The resistance, holed up in underground bunkers, plants roadside bombs and ambushes isolated German units. Its members are told in advance that they can expect to survive on average for two weeks. But they have, as Enoch Powell would have put it, a country to die for in their heroic defiance of this Nazified United Europe.

In C. J. Sansom's 2012 novel *Dominion*, another best-selling English thriller based on a successful Nazi takeover in 1940, after a British surrender at Dunkirk, we find speculation in 1952, when the novel is set, that 'the Queen's Coronation next year will be in some way combined with celebrations of the twentieth anniversary of Herr Hitler's accession to power in Germany' – the most potent drama of British sovereignty re-imagined as a grotesque puppet show, majesty turned to subjection. In his bibliographical note Sansom notes, 'In looking at how a British Resistance movement might have fought a collaborationist regime, the closest (though not exact) parallel has to be the French Resistance.'[42] (Sansom's book was animated in particular by fear of Scottish independence, and its depiction of a pro-Nazi collaborationist Scottish National Party in 1952 is explicitly aimed at discouraging support for the contemporary SNP – in an appendix, he directly urges readers to donate to and support the 'No' campaign in the impending referendum of 2014.)

The pay-off for all of this lurid imagining would come with Brexit. In February 2016, when David Cameron was seeking concessions from Brussels in advance of the Brexit referendum, the *Daily Mail*, forgetting its own history of appeasement, brazenly compared him to Neville Chamberlain in a rabid front-page editorial headed, of course 'Who will speak for England?'[43] (While drawing these parallels between the Nazis and the EU, it added in the smaller print, 'Nobody is suggesting there are any parallels whatever between the Nazis and the EU.')

The Leave.EU campaign ran images of Chelsea Pensioners with the slogan 'Freedom and democracy. Let's not give up values for which our ancestors fought.'[44] Its funder Arron Banks claimed he was handed a letter and donation for £30 by a Second World War veteran: 'I am an old soldier from the last war. I remember the French and Belgians in 1940, what we called the surrender monkeys… who we saved. My father was an Old Contemptible in France in 1914. He says you can't trust them and they proved him right. We were never thanked.' (The old veteran was a far-seeing visionary, or perhaps just a fan of *The Simpsons*, where the term 'surrender monkey' was invented in 1995.)

The most peculiar result of all of this strange history of imagining the EU as really a front for a German plot to achieve by stealth what Hitler had failed to achieve by force came in the immediate period after the referendum. If you've thrilled yourself with these dark imaginings you end with the ultimate in wish-fulfilment: the EU is a front for a German cabal *and this will save Brexit*. It is hard to overstate the extent to which Brexit depended on the idea of who *really* runs the EU: German car manufacturers. For some of those at the top of the Labour Party, the idea of the EU as a mere front for the bosses and moguls of Europe was a reason to be secretly pleased that Brexit would allow Britain to escape their clutches and build socialism in one country. But on the Tory Right, the German moguls were, for a brief shining moment, not oppressors but saviours. David Davis said during the referendum campaign that 'the first calling point of the UK's negotiator in the time immediately after Brexit will not be Brussels, it will be Berlin to strike the deal. Absolute access for German cars and industrial goods in exchange for a sensible deal on everything else.' A year after the referendum, when Davis was the UK's lead negotiator as secretary of state for Brexit, Andrew Marr put it to him: 'You basically argued that the German car industry, and German industry generally, would put pressure on the German chancellor who would put pressure on the EU to ensure that we got a good deal. Is that still your view?' 'Oh,' replied Davis, 'that's where it will end up, yeah.'

Boris Johnson was even more explicit in the BBC's big setpiece final debate before the referendum in June 2016. 'Everyone knows this country receives about one-fifth of Germany's entire car manufacturing output,' he said. 'Do you seriously propose that they are going to be so insane as to allow tariffs to be imposed?' The key word here is 'allow'. How telling it is. It reveals an entire view of how the world really works. Even while Brexit was posing as an exercise in returning control to the populace, Johnson was letting slip his understanding of where control really lay. The chain of reasoning began with a factual proposition: the Germans sell a hell of a lot of cars to the UK. The next link in the chain is rational: therefore, the German car manufacturers would not want any tariff barriers to be created after Brexit. And then there is the great leap. Seeing their interests threatened, the bosses of Mercedes and Audi would lift the phone to the chancellery. 'Merkel!' they would bark. 'There must be no tariff barriers. We will not allow it!' Angela Merkel in turn would call Jean-Claude Juncker and Donald Tusk: 'The British must have their cake and eat it. Understood?' 'Jawohl!' BMW means Brexit Made Wonderful.

In part, this stems from a most rarefied political plant: Tory Marxism. Edward St Aubyn epitomized it in *Some Hope*: 'They're the last Marxists... The last people who believe that class is a total explanation. Long after that doctrine has been abandoned in Moscow and Peking it will continue to flourish under the marquees of England. Although most of them have the courage of a half-eaten worm... and the intellectual vigour of dead sheep, they are the true heirs of Marx and Lenin.'[45] In an elitist view of the world, rules would not matter. The EU's institutions were Potemkin villages, flimsy and easily knocked over. Brexit would, naturally, be settled behind the scenes by unelected power-brokers. Merkel would do as she was told and, as the EU is a German front, Brussels would snap its heels and produce the proper offer of infinite cake.

That this belonged in the realm of an imaginary construct is obvious from its most glaring contradiction: if the German car bosses could order Merkel to produce a lovely Brexit for Britain, why could the British car bosses, who opposed Brexit, not stop it altogether? The answer, of course, is that all of this resulted from a fantasy about Germany and the EU that had been played out in books, films and tabloid fictions. This was the final stage of the delusion, the one where self-pity becomes pure pleasure. The idea of German oppression had always carried a charge of erotic satisfaction. Now, it would deliver its full load of bliss: secret German domination would save Brexit and open the way to the easiest and best deal in history.

It didn't, of course, so then there was the rage of further disappointed expectations. From being saviours, the Germans turned back into the Nazis of *SS-GB*. The rabidly pro-Brexit *Express* screamed in November 2017: 'German MEP demands "unconditional SURRENDER" from UK for Brexit talks to progress', the opening line of the article turning this into a demand by the EU itself: 'The EU is demanding "unconditional surrender" and an agreement on a £53 billion divorce bill by next Friday before starting trade negotiations.'[46] The equally intransigent *Telegraph* carried similar headlines: 'Germany expects Brexit secretary David Davis to offer his "unconditional surrender" to the EU's terms when he delivers a keynote speech to trade chiefs in Berlin on Thursday evening, the former president of the country's largest trade body has warned.'[47] And the *Sun*: 'PUT EU HANDS UP. Berlin wants Britain's unconditional surrender in Brexit talks, claims German official.'[48] The UKIP MEP Gerald Batten claimed that

'The Commission wants unconditional surrender and Mrs May will settle for conditional surrender.'[49]

The long-running fantasy of imagining 'we had suffered defeat in a war' became explicit in the Brexit talks. The Tory MEP Daniel Hannan tweeted in February 2018: 'Throughout the negotiations, HMG has adopted a friendly and respectful tone. The Brussels institutions respond as if dealing with a hostile power.'[50] Hannan further ramped up the metaphorical 'as if' in outrage at the failure of the EU to accept Theresa May's Chequers plan wholesale: 'No British government could go further to accommodate the EU. If Brussels holds out for more, dictating terms *as if to a defeated enemy* (my italics), a breakdown is inevitable.'[51]

As though we had suffered defeat in a war, dictating terms as if to a defeated enemy – there is here a kind of wish-fulfilment. This desire to experience the vicarious thrills of humiliation is possible only in a country that did not know what national humiliation is really like. But the problem with wish-fulfilment is that your wishes might end up being fulfilled. In the Brexit negotiations, the idea of national humiliation moved from fiction to reality. There was a strange ecstasy of shame: 'Britain faces a terrible choice: between the humiliation of a deal dictated by Brussels; and the chaos of crashing out of the EU';[52] 'A week from hell: How Theresa May's *Panorama* positivity turned to humiliation in Salzburg';[53] 'Failed clean Brexit would be biggest "national humiliation" since the Suez crisis, MPs will warn';[54] 'Humiliation beckons if we cannot unite around a plan for Brexit';[55] 'Salzburg humiliation leaves May idling at the Brexit crossroads';[56] 'Cabinet at war after May's humiliation in

Salzburg';[57] 'Humiliation for May as EU rejects Brexit plan'.[58]

With Brexit, England would experience the consequences of not being careful what you wish for.

3.

THE TRIUMPH OF
THE LIGHT BRIGADE

Lose, and start again at your beginnings
And never breathe a word about your loss

—RUDYARD KIPLING

I n September 2016, less than three months after the Brexit referendum, marine researchers manoeuvred a small, remotely operated vehicle through the open hatch of a ship that was lying on the bottom of an Arctic bay. They guided it through a mess hall and found a storage room with plates and a can still sitting on one of the shelves. 'We spotted two wine bottles, tables and empty shelving. Found a desk with open drawers with something in the back corner of the drawer,' the director of the operation, Adrian Schimnowski, told the *Guardian* in an email.[1] They had discovered something that the British Admiralty had once spent a long time looking for: the wreck of HMS *Terror*, one of two ships lost in Sir John

Franklin's doomed attempt to find the Northwest Passage in 1848. Franklin's expedition, in which all 129 men were lost, was by far the worst disaster in the history of British polar exploration. It was also one of the great episodes in the British cult of heroic failure. The timing could hardly have been more exquisite, for just as dreams of Nazi occupation channelled one aspect of England's sense of loss – the disappointment of victory in the war – heroic failure spoke to the other, the strange legacy of colonialism. It provides a small window into the second form of self-pity that goes into the making of Brexit: the colonizer imagining itself as the colonized.

Franklin was, as Stephanie Barczewski puts it in her richly illuminating history *Heroic Failure and the British*, 'a failure on a monumental scale, but he nonetheless became one of the greatest Victorian heroes'.[2] Indeed, Franklin's story is one of repeated debacle. On his first voyage to find the Northwest Passage in 1819 and 1820, he had to abandon his ship and nine of his twenty men died, 'some at the hands of others, who were so desperate for food that they resorted to cannibalism'. Yet, on his return to England, Franklin's journal of the expedition became a best-seller, hailed as a 'splendid display of those noble qualities which seem particularly distinctive of the Saxon race'.[3] This was surely true – Franklin had a particular genius for appealing to the most transformative faculty in the English imagination, the imperial alchemy that turned the lead of disaster into the gold of heroism.

His second expedition in 1845 was deeply Brexitlike. As Barczewski explains, it was undertaken in a spirit of blithe optimism: 'Nothing could be simpler. But the plan ignored the fact that 500 miles (800 km) of the voyage were unmapped, meaning that the actual distance that a ship needed to travel might prove much longer as it picked its way through ice and the Arctic archipelago. This had not mattered in the imaginations of the journey's planners.'[4] If this sounds awfully familiar to anyone who has watched the course of Brexit's voyage from 'nothing could be simpler' to getting lost in unmapped wastelands, it may be because the same attitudes have been at work.

The tragicomic outcome was not just that Franklin and his men were lost but that enormous amounts of effort and money were expended on trying to find them. It became a Victorian obsession: over the next decade a total of thirty-eight public and private expeditions, mostly from Britain, but also from the United States and Russia, went to the Arctic to search for Franklin. By 1854, the Admiralty alone had spent £600,000 (tens of millions in today's values) looking for Franklin. 'Some of the rescue expeditions had themselves had to be rescued.'[5] Heroic failure acted like a magnet, drawing ever more failure towards itself.

But what is even more Brexitlike is the idea that those who ventured out to find Franklin, even if they endured terrible hardships, were seen to have failed, not because the enterprise itself was mad, but because they were insufficiently determined. Lieutenant Sherard Osborn, who led an expedition in 1851, survived vicious storms and brought his men home safe. He was taken aback by his reception when he returned: 'Our self-importance as Arctic heroes of the first water received a sad downfall when we were first asked by a kind friend what the deuce we came home for?... and why we deserted Franklin?'[6] Ironically, when one of the expeditions, led by Robert McClure, did in fact find the entrance to the Northwest Passage, the discovery was virtually ignored. He did not find Franklin and mere reality had long since ceased to matter. No doubt British civil servants trying to map the route to the least damaging Brexit would know exactly how he felt – complicated realities are no match for the glamour of heroic failure.

A crucial difference, though, is that in the traditional English idea of heroic failure, the great point is *not* to feel self-pity. England's favourite poem, Rudyard Kipling's 'If', tells us that Triumph and Disaster are essentially indistinguishable, 'two impostors just the same' – a dangerous lesson for a country whose future hangs on the ability to tell the difference. But it also enjoins the English to 'lose, and start again at your beginnings/ And never breathe a word about your loss'. Losing everything – even life itself – and not whining about it is the traditional English ideal of courage. As Barczewski has it 'the highest form of English heroism is stoicism in the face of failure'.[7]

This is the last thing anyone would say about the conduct of Brexit. The only stiff upper lips on display in England now belong to the victims of botched Botox jobs. In a coincidence in its own way as resonant as the finding of HMS *Terror*, the Royal Mail issued in June 2018, when the Brexit project was in deepest disarray, a set of stamps to mark the fiftieth anniversary of the first screening of the long-running and perennially popular wartime sitcom *Dad's Army*. One of the stamps has the catchphrase 'Don't panic! Don't panic!' printed on a still from the series of Clive Dunn's elderly Home Guard soldier, Lance Corporal Jones, mouth agape, glasses askew and, of course, in an awful funk.

Brexit has been much more *Dad's Army* than 'If', more Corporal Jones than Scott of the Antarctic. Derek Mahon's great poem 'Antarctica' encapsulates the self-sacrifice of Scott's companion, Lawrence Oates, who walked quietly out into the snow to die uttering the immortal line, 'I am just going outside and may be some time.'

The others nod, pretending not to know.
At the heart of the ridiculous, the sublime.

It is an acknowledgement that there is, after all, a heroism in heroic failure. But Brexit reverses the order. It occupies this psychic territory but turns its tragic sensibility into farce – at the heart of its sublime the ridiculous.

The grand balls-up is not new, and in English historical memory it is not shameful. Most of the modern English heroes, after all, are complete screw-ups. The exploits that have loomed largest in English consciousness since the nineteenth century are retreats or disasters: Sir John Moore's evacuation of Corunna in the Peninsular War, the Charge of the Light Brigade, the doomed Franklin expedition, 'Scott of the Antarctic', the 'last stand' against the Zulus at Isandlwana, Gordon of Khartoum, the Somme, the flight from Dunkirk. This culture of heroic failure Barczewski defines as 'a conscious sense of celebration of the striving for an object that was not attained'. She points, for example, to the ten memorial statues in Waterloo Place, a key site flanking the great processional route up the Mall towards Buckingham Palace: five relate to the disastrous Crimean War, one is of Franklin and one is of Captain Robert Falcon Scott, who died with four of his men having failed to get to the South Pole before Roald Amundsen's pragmatically planned and unromantic Norwegian expedition.

The essence of English heroic failure is Scott reflecting on his own fast-approaching death at the Antarctic: 'We took risks, we knew we took them. Things have come out against us, and therefore we have no cause for complaint, but bow to the will of Providence, determined still to do our best to the last... Had we lived, I should have had a tale to tell of the hardihood, endurance and courage of my companions which would have stirred the heart of every Englishman. These rough notes and our dead bodies must tell the tale.'[8]

There is something genuinely magnificent in this English capacity to embrace disaster. It is also highly creative. It trans-forms ugly facts into beautiful fantasies. The charge of the Light Brigade was a hideous fiasco. At the Battle of Balaclava in the Crimean War in October 1854, the British cavalry charged, sabres aloft, at the Russian artillery, down a long valley that was also flanked by Russian guns that could fire on them from above. It was pure, suicidal butchery: survivors wrote things like 'never was such murder ordered'; 'Thank God I escaped that dreadful massacre', 'a horrible sight for any human being to witness'. Lieutenant Fiennes Wykeham Martin wrote to his brother: 'My Regiment is cut up and the rest of the Light Brigade are completely annihilated owing to a mistake in the orders... Of 700 men who went into action only 190 came out and all for no good...'⁹ But the prime minister Lord Palmerston described it as 'glorious' and Alfred Tennyson wrote a poem that every schoolboy and schoolgirl, even of my generation in republican Ireland, knew: 'Theirs not to make reply,/ Theirs not to reason why,/ Theirs but to do and die.'

George Orwell noted in 1941 that Tennyson's poem still epitomized popular English patriotism: 'English literature, like other literatures, is full of battle-poems, but it is worth noticing that the ones that have won for themselves a kind of popularity are always a tale of disasters and retreats. There is no popular poem about Trafalgar or Waterloo, for instance... The most stirring battle-poem in English is all about a brigade of cavalry which charged in the wrong direction.'

He continued, sombrely, to evoke the more recent memory of the Great War: 'the four names which have really engraved themselves on the popular memory are Mons, Ypres, Gallipoli and Passchendaele, every time a disaster. The names of the great battles that finally broke the German armies are simply unknown to the general public.'¹⁰

The problem now, however, is that the original English cult of heroic failure was, paradoxically, a symptom of British power. As Barczewski astutely notes: 'Heroic failure... neither effected nor engendered decline; on the contrary it arose from British power and dominance, and from the need to provide alternative narratives that distracted from its real-life exploitative and violent aspects.' The English could afford to celebrate glorious failure because they were actually highly successful – the myths of suffering and endurance covered up the truth that it was mostly other people who had to endure the suffering.

Heroic failure was an exercise in transference. The British needed to fill a yawning gap between their self-image as exemplars of liberty and civility and the violence and domination that were the realities of Empire. Some of this could be done by absorbing defeated peoples into the heroic image of the imperial army: the Gaels of the Scottish Highlands, finally crushed in the eighteenth century, or the Gurkhas of Nepal subdued after vicious fighting in the nineteenth. Some could be done by the method Orwell ascribed to most of the English working class: deliberately 'not knowing that the Empire exists'.[11] But heroic failure was an even more powerful mechanism for assuaging guilt: it reimagined the British conquest of the earth as an epic of suffering, not for the victims, but for the victors. It took the pain of the oppressed and ascribed it to the oppressors.

It had to be understood, of course, that heroic failure was not to be treated as an admission of weakness. On the face of it, celebrating disasters seems to be advertising one's capacity for screwing up. It ought to have invited ridicule, all this getting lost in wildernesses, heading off with bad maps, failing to make plans, not delivering vital messages, sending the cavalry off to charge in the wrong direction. To turn it into a statement of strength, it was crucial that there be no self-pity. Indeed, it was not simply that there must be no self-pity – this absence must itself be supremely present. This is how strong we are: even in the face of disaster we don't cry, we don't complain, we don't stop to reason why and we never breathe a word about our loss. We are going out now and we may be some time.

This is possible only when you are in fact confident of your superiority. Subject cultures have heroic failures – the Battle of Kosovo for the Serbs, the Easter Rising for the Irish – but they dramatize them and saturate them in grief. In its original form, the English cult is not like this at all. It doesn't have to worry about long-term outcomes, for those will all be successful: the Zulus will be beaten, the Russians will lose the war. Its concern, instead, is with *character*. Heroic failure became such an important part of British culture because it celebrated personal virtues that were understood to be at the core of national identity and encapsulated in that most English of English words: pluck. It was not about achieving, it was about *being* – being male and upper class but also being stoical, cool, resilient, uncomplaining, able to endure everything that nature or barbaric peoples could inflict. The personal in this sense was deeply political: a man so utterly in control of himself earned the right to control others.

But what do you do with this habit of mind when you are no longer superior, when you can't afford to indulge your inherited tastes for grandiose bungling, when your ruling class can't control even its own buffoonery, but you still have a sweet tooth for these empty calories of heroic failure? In some respects, Brexit is a perfect vehicle for this zombie cult. It fuses three of the archetypes of heroic English failure. There is the last stand, exemplified by the death of General George Gordon at Khartoum, another fiasco that quickly became a byword for heroism in the face of inevitable disaster: Brexit is imperial England's *last* last stand. There is the suicidal cavalry charge: the Brexiteers in the heady early days of 2017, threatening

Europe that if it does not play nice they will destroy its economic artillery with their flashing sabres. And there is the doomed expedition without a map into a terra incognita that is also a promised land. Yet as heroic exits go, it is not like that of Captain Oates.

The difficulty lies with the question of transference – what is being transferred to whom? In its prime, the cult was, in many ways, the ultimate colonial appropriation. Britain took to itself, not just the resources of the conquered people, but their suffering and endurance. In its Brexit iteration, it has to take this much further: to imagine the greatest colonial power in modern history as itself a colony. This is in its own way quite audacious – England dreaming itself into the status it so triumphantly imposed on others. It is a dramatic bypass operation. In reality, Britain went from being an imperial power to being a reasonably ordinary but privileged Western European country. In the apparition conjured by Brexit, it went straight from being the colonizer to being the colonized.

There is a kind of bridge between the two states: the Dunkirk spirit. It was another surreal coincidence that Christopher Nolan's epic and vivid movie of the most recent and potent episode of heroic failure hit the screens in 2017, in perfect time to function as a Brexit metaphor. But this is a metaphor that has one leg in heroism, the other in a kind of grandiose banality.

In the early years of the UK's membership of the Common Market, 'Dunkirk spirit' could be used ironically, with a knowing anti-heroic twist. A cartoon in *Punch* in 1974, commenting on the exodus of Brits to Australia, shows an official at the Australian embassy in London processing a vast queue of would-be emigrants: 'They're beginning to show their Dunkirk spirit – They're even willing to go in small boats.'[12] But by the time of the fortieth anniversary of the evacuation, its mythical status as a crucible of English character had been fully re-established. As Robert Harris wrote in May 1990, 'It was and is an affirmation of our insularity... Our future may lie on the Continent. Our hearts are still in the past, in a mythical world of "little ships" delivering gallant Tommies from the clutches of perfidious, cowardly foreigners.'[13]

The continuing potency of this myth is embodied in Nolan's film through Mark Rylance's moving performance as Mr Dawson, the ordinary Englishman who skippers his own small yacht across the Channel and carries back dozens of men while evading German fighters. Rylance, tellingly, had already incarnated one half of the English male self-image in his sensational stage performance as the Falstaffian Rooster Byron in Jez Butterworth's *Jerusalem* – the strutting, antic, anarchic side of popular Toryism. In *Dunkirk* he inhabits the other half, the silent, undemonstrative heroic endurance of danger and suffering. He has very few lines and the ones he has are as clipped as anything from Captain Scott or Lawrence Oates – we can quite imagine him saying as he sets out to sea that he is sailing off now and may be some time. He gives nothing away – we do not even learn his first name. But we can guess that he surely endured the Great War and we learn that he has himself lost a son already in this war.

In Rylance's great performance all this is etched on his face and sunk in the pools of sorrow behind his eyes. It is emphatically not expressed as self-pity – indeed, it vividly re-creates the grand age of English heroism in which self-pity functions as a radiant absence. And it is deeply affecting, so much so that it is possible to believe while watching it that this whole tradition is still alive and politically serviceable, that Brexit itself can somehow be imbued with its superbly tacit glamour, that it, too, can evoke a notion of English suffering that is not saturated in self-pity.

The problem is that the evocation of Dunkirk in real, contemporary English life is the very opposite. It is indeed a prime example of the self-pity inherent in self-dramatizing exaggeration. It is where wartime heroics meets tourism: every large-scale interruption to the travel plans of Brits is, in the media, a new Dunkirk. In 1980, for example, protesting French trawlermen blockaded ports. *The Economist* reported: 'The Dunkirk spirit, good and not so good, lives again. Dashing British ferry-boat captains ran the French trawlermen's blockade of northern French ports; a truce was arranged and 20,000 never-say-die British tourists wriggled out of strike-bound French harbours after effectively being held hostage for several days. British newspapers quoted *Henry V*.'[14]

In 2010, when the explosion of a volcano in Iceland caused chaos for travellers, the *Financial Times* wrote that 'stranded travellers summoned the Dunkirk spirit to try to get home by bicycle, ferry, powerboat, container ship, or whatever means they could'.[15] The *Daily Star* kept its readers' spirits up with a stirring tale: 'BBC newsreader Tim Willcox, 46, was left stranded in Egypt after a holiday with wife Sarah, 39, and children Sophia, 13, George 11, and Tom, eight. He got a flight to Barcelona, then hired a taxi for £300 to take him to Perpignan,

France, where he rented a car. Tim, who was driving the family to Calais last night, said: "I will be more than £1,000 out of pocket – but at least there is a real Dunkirk spirit."'[16]

In 2012, when some British passengers were on a cruise ship on which a (very minor) fire had broken out, the *Sunday Express*, under the headline 'Dunkirk spirit of cruise Brits', announced: 'British passengers, among more than 1,000 people onboard a stricken cruise ship adrift in Philippine waters... have been showing the "Dunkirk spirit". Jeremy Scott said his parents, Valerie and Billy Scott, who are on the *Azamara Quest*, rang him yesterday in Pinner, Middlesex, to tell him they were "fine". "There is no panic, everybody is fine. It's the Dunkirk spirit and they are making the best of the situation."'[17] When 'Mum and Dad are fine' (which is the substance of this story) merits a triple dose of Dunkirk spirit, the currency of heroic failure is deeply debased.

This is, as we shall see, much more typical of the Brexit mentality. Mr Dawson's 'Dunkirk spirit' is all about understatement – verbal and emotional. It is a great holding back. The 'Dunkirk spirit' that chimes with Brexit is all overstatement – verbal and emotional. It is a great letting go. The grand tradition is a kind of *sprezzatura*, a studied indifference in which deep feeling expresses itself as nonchalance. It takes big things – appalling suffering and death – and cuts them down to size. The new 'Dunkirk spirit' is a kind of hysteria in which the ordinary vicissitudes of life (especially those involving Brits abroad among foreigners) are raised to the level of epic suffering. It is a long way from Robert Falcon Scott in the Antarctic to Valerie and Billy Scott on the *Azamara Quest* – the distance between heroic failure as a subtle advertisement of true power and as a compensation for actual weakness. But the end point of the journey would be reached in September 2018, when foreign secretary Jeremy Hunt warned the Europeans that they would be very sorry indeed if they continued to insult Britain by not giving it the Brexit it was demanding: 'The way Britain reacts is not that we crumble or fold but actually you end up invoking the Dunkirk spirit and we fight back… We are one of the great countries of Europe and there comes a point where we say "we're not prepared to be pushed around, if you're not serious about a deal then we won't be either".'[18]

John Cleese wrote in his autobiography about being taken with his entire school to see the Ealing Studios film *Scott of the Antarctic* in 1948:

> We were all deeply impressed by Scott's uncomplaining acceptance of suffering. But you couldn't help feeling that the message of the film was not just that the highest form of English heroism is stoicism in the face of failure but that in Scott's case a whiff of success might have tarnished the gallantry of his silent endurance of misery… in the same way that the magnificence of the Charge of the Light Brigade was enhanced by its utter futility, and General Gordon's being calmly hacked to death was all the more impressive because it occurred during the complete annihilation of his forces at Khartoum.[19]

It seems somehow apt that less than thirty years after being impressed by Scott's uncomplaining endurance, Cleese gave the world an alternative image of Englishness that seems in retrospect more representative of the culture that produced Brexit: a hysterical Basil Fawlty giving a 'damn good thrashing' to his broken-down Austin 1100 Countryman Estate with the branch of a tree.

If the point of the cult of heroic failure was to disguise the realities of colonial dominance, it required radical adjustment in the post-imperial context of British membership of the EU. It had to let in the self-pity it had always held at bay. And it did this in the most startling way: by imagining Britain itself as a colony of the EU, a plucky little nation with its own deep traditions that had been annexed by a European superstate. The idea of resistance to this superstate could, as we have seen, plug itself into memories of wartime resistance movements. But an even more powerful generator was the idea of an anti-colonial liberation movement – the very movements that the British had previously sought to crush.

It seems right that, in the early summer of 2018, as Britain's talks with the EU about withdrawal and future relations were becoming increasingly futile, David Nicholls' five-part TV adaptation of Edward St Aubyn's Patrick Melrose novels was being screened. The novels are about sadism and masochism – the monstrously sadistic father David and the self-harming behaviour of the son he abused. They unfold in a context that is both upper class and post-imperial – in the first episode of the TV series we see Benedict Cumberbatch's Patrick in a suicidal frenzy of drug-taking in an extremely expensive hotel, while Cy Endfield's 1964 movie Zulu, which begins with the great heroic failure of Islandlwana, plays on the television.

This is a subliminal preview of David's sermon on the infliction of pain as an act of love, which also appropriates the suffering of a defeated and colonized people. Before he sexually abuses his son for the first time, David will tell him: 'King Shaka was a great and mighty Zulu warrior who made his troops stamp thorn bushes into the ground and march for days across hot, jagged rocks. The soles of their feet were slashed and burnt. And though there was resentment and pain at the time, the calluses this created meant that eventually, nothing would harm them. They would feel no pain. And what had felt like cruelty at the time was actually a gift. It was actually love.'

This draws on a whole history of sadomasochistic imperial education, the toughening-up of white children by savage cruelty in public schools so that they can in turn inflict themselves on lesser peoples. In Jane Gardam's novel *Old Filth*, Babs remembers, of this form of education, that 'The complaining ones were thought to be cowards. We had to copy the Spartans in those days. You should have seen the illustrations in children's books of the Raj then. Pictures of children beating *each other* with canes at school. The prefectorial system. Now it would be thought porn.'[20]

But David Melrose's parable goes even deeper: he takes the pain of the defeated Zulus and transfers it into his own son's body and mind by abusing him. This taking on of colonial pain is nothing like a coherent idea. Indeed, the fundamental contradiction of Brexit is that it wants to think of itself simultaneously as a reconstitution of Empire and as an anti-imperial national liberation movement. On the one side, it evokes the idea of a new mercantilist dominion reuniting the old imperial realm as a British-centred trading zone with India, Australia, Canada and indeed African countries all delighted to offer fabulous trade deals to the still-beloved Mother Country, an idea dryly described by sceptical Whitehall officials as 'Empire 2.0'.[21] On the other, it sacralizes 23 June 2016 as, in Nigel Farage's coinage, Independence Day – a term that hitherto belonged to the ex-colonies: June 2016 as England's own Easter 1916. Immediately after hailing the day of the Brexit referendum in these terms, Farage added: 'We'll have done it without having to fight, without a single bullet being fired.' The implication, even in the negative, was that the EU was the kind of colonizing power that other countries had typically had to overthrow in wars of independence.

The very title of a key manifesto – *Britannia Unchained* – evoked images of enslavement. It was published in 2012 by five then-rising stars of the Tory Party, most of whom would end up in cabinet. One of them, Dominic Raab, would in July 2018 become secretary of state for Brexit. Strikingly, the book begins with a dystopian evocation of the London riots of August 2011 – but with a startling insistence on all Britain's problems being embodied by a young black man, Beau Isagba, who was filmed attacking a young Malaysian student and later jailed: 'Sadly, Beau Isagba represents the worst of what some elements of Britain have become.'[22] The young Tories go on to revive the narrative of post-imperial decline, a weakening of the moral fibre evident in protest: 'a spirit of decline has returned... Radical political views are gaining support. Agonised navel-gazing is now the fashion, debating the distribution of growth, rather than how to grow the economy as a whole. Hundreds camped in the "Occupy London" protests outside St Paul's Cathedral in the autumn of 2011.'[23] At the heart of this malaise is the rather dimly perceived connection between loss of Empire and the sustainability of the United Kingdom: 'Britain once ruled the Empire on which the sun never set. Now it can barely keep England and Scotland together.'

In this self-pitying mood, there is final reversal of colonial stereotypes. Under Empire, it was the natives who were lazy, shiftless, slavishly dependent, inherently inclined to criminality. Now, England itself has succumbed to this disease. Deprived of imperial grandeur, John Bull has become Beau Isagba. It is the former colonial subjects who are now what the English once were – striving, disciplined, ambitious – while the English have adopted their old ways: 'Once they enter the workplace, the British are among the worst idlers in the world. We work among the lowest hours, we retire early and our productivity is poor. Whereas Indian children aspire to be doctors or businessmen, the British are more interested in football and pop music.'[24]

How can this reversal, in which the old mother country has become the colonial brat, be itself reversed? By doing what the former colonies did – 'unchaining' themselves. In part this is a call to complete the neoliberal project of complete deregulation. *Britannia Unchained* evokes the piratical buccaneers whose private pursuit of wealth forged the Empire – one chapter is in fact called 'Buccaneers' and quotes approvingly from Steve Jobs: 'It's more fun to be a pirate than to join the navy.' The authors grudgingly concede that 'law and order' is 'on the whole beneficial' but make little effort to conceal that their hearts are with 'capitalism as chaos' and the magic that happens in the former colonies when 'when nearly all society's strictures are relaxed'.[25] Here is the final turning upside-down of Empire. Once, the colonized peoples required the smack of firm British rule because, left to themselves, they were ungovernable. Now it is this very ungovernability that the old mother country must learn from its former subjects. In chaos capitalism, it is not a disease to be cured but a consummation devoutly to be wished. And this consummation can be achieved, not when the old colonies rejoin the Empire, but when the old imperial power rejoins them. British children will be released from their enslavement to welfare dependency only when they become Indian.

What is remarkable, given that the authors will become supporters of Brexit, and in Raab's case be charged with actually making it happen, is that in this fantasy of a reverse-engineered Empire the EU barely features at all. Britain's relationship to it is explicitly mentioned just once: 'Britain is increasingly isolated from the European Union.'[26] There is a very vague feeling that Britain, in order to recover the buccaneering spirit of the early Empire, must step outside 'the cosy European tent'.[27] But here again we see the real dynamic of Brexit – the oppressive EU as a necessary invention. The point, even in 2012, is the act of unchaining oneself and in order to be unchained it is necessary to have a master to be unchained *from*.

This in turn opens up the idea that 'Empire 2.0' was really a dream, not just of leaving the EU, but of putting the old white empire back together again in the shape of the Anglo-Saxon Union envisaged by Robert Conquest in 1971 and subsequently reimagined as the Anglosphere. The use of Independence Day as a way of framing Brexit was intended to appeal primarily to Americans, who are familiar with 4th July as their own Independence Day holiday, marking the adoption of the Declaration of Independence. There are, however, two big problems with this neo-imperial project. One is that even the most deluded Brexiteer would concede that even if it were ever to come about, its centre would not be in London but in Washington. It would be an American, not a British empire. George Orwell had long ago anticipated it in *Nineteen Eighty-Four*, where it essentially exists as Oceania. It is not good news for England, which is now called Airstrip One. Even as pure fantasy, which it is, the Anglo-Saxon Union does not set the pulses racing – liberation from a marginal position in one empire to a marginal position in another is not much of a thrill.

Secondly, the imperial idea has little appeal to the working-class English voters who are crucial to Brexit. It is their children who died or who live with PTSD after the fag-end British imperial Anglospheric adventures in Iraq and Afghanistan. And the realities of England becoming a satellite of the US, even if sweetened with delusions of getting the old white imperial gang back together, are, for English workers, even further exposure to the very disruptions of neoliberal globalization from which they are seeking shelter. If the Anglo-Saxon Union comes in the shape of chlorinated chicken and the dismantling of workers' rights, it doesn't cut it even as a phantasmagorical spectre.

But there is an even more pressing reason why the idea of Britain as a colony breaking the chains of imperial oppression has far greater urgency than the notion of Britain as the mouse rising once more on the back of the American eagle. Brexit came to the boil in the midst of a wider turmoil of far-right nationalism. And in that stew, a crucial ingredient is the transference of victimhood: the claim that white men, rather than being (as they are) relatively privileged, are in fact victims. Victimhood has been seen to be the currency of power – women, people of colour, ethnic minorities appeal for equality by reference to their collective suffering. In this sense, the far-right is the white man's #MeToo movement. Not only am I not guilty, but I am in fact a victim.

Self-pity is not to be guarded against in this cultural moment – it *is* the moment. Brexit is about many things but one of them is the feeling that there is a much larger rot to stop, a natural order of things that is being eroded by feminism, multi-culturalism, immigration, globalization and Islam. Emotionally, Brexit is fuelled by anxiety. Asked on the eve of the referendum how EU membership made them *feel*, voters were given a list of eight words, four positive (happy, hopeful, confident, proud) and four negative (angry, uneasy, disgusted, afraid) and invited to choose up to four of them. Feelings of 'unease' dominated, with 44 per cent selecting this word, as against just 26 per cent who went for the most popular positive term, 'hopeful'. No other positive word was selected by more than 14 per cent. Overall, just 32 per cent chose one or more positive words, while fully 50 per cent chose one or more negative words. Twice as many felt angry as felt happy.[28]

The great salve to anxiety is the sense of control. The Brexit campaign spoke directly to this need with its brilliant slogan: Take Back Control. But this is exactly what the grand tradition of British heroic failure would never have articulated. There could be no 'back' about it. Its fundamental gesture was: I as an English gentleman – and thus by extension we English – *am* in control. Brexit in this sense has to concede a great deal of psychological ground. It cannot afford the supreme self-confidence of treating triumph and disaster as twin imposters. Where the grand tradition laughs in the face of fear, Brexit had to tap into deep anxiety about the loss of status. It had to somehow put together two fears – the older one about Britain's loss of status in the world after 1945 and the newer concern that the privileges of whiteness were being eroded.

For people who feel anxious about the threat of losing their status, self-pity is attractive because it combines righteous anger with reassurance. You are reassured because you know you deserve a great deal, righteously angry because for some reason you have not been getting what you so obviously deserve. This combination has always been alluring to anti-colonial liberation movements: we are a great, unique people therefore we deserve to be free; only the colonial oppressor is preventing us from enjoying the freedom we deserve. Brexit steals these clothes. It is a *Trading Places* movie in which all the complications, disappointments and restrictions of being a former colonial power can be exchanged for the exuberant victimhood of anti-colonial resistance.

Perhaps the strangest expression of this is the desire of mainstream Tory Brexiteers to place themselves in, of all things, the narrative of Irish history. Odd as it is, it has precedents in literature. In the best anatomy of the sadomasochistic psychology of a decadent British ruling class, St Aubyn's Patrick

Melrose saga, there is an especially audacious imaginative reversal of history. The Irish nineteenth century was characterized by the catastrophe of the Great Famine of the 1840s, mass eviction of the poorest tenant farmers and their forced emigration to the United States. St Aubyn replays this upside-down – the key event in the novels is the eviction of the English upper-class family from its beloved chateau *by the Irish*. The manipulative Irish interloper Seamus manages to take over Melrose's home. He specifically evokes the Famine in explaining his concept of prosperity: "'Ultimately, it's having something to eat when you're hungry. That's the prosperity that was denied to Ireland, for instance, during the 1840s...'" "Gosh", said Mary. "There's not a lot I can do about the Irish in the 1840s.'" Shortly after this exchange, the conflict comes to a head with the horrible consequence that the Melroses are both turfed out of their chateau and forced to go (for their annual holidays) to America instead: '"America", said Robert. "I want to go to America." "Why not?" said Patrick. "That's where Europeans traditionally go when they've been evicted."'[29]

Equally, in C. J. Sansom's *Dominion*, the collaborationist British government, created in London after the surrender at Dunkirk in 1940, deploys the Special Branch Auxiliaries: 'When they were first created in the 1940s to deal with growing civil unrest, David's father had said the Auxiliaries reminded him of the Black and Tans, the violent trench veterans recruited by Lloyd George to augment the police during the Irish Independence War. All were armed.' They are referred to later in the book as 'the Auxies', the precise nickname given to the Auxiliaries sent to put down the IRA in Ireland. Conversely,

Sansom's protagonist, David Fitzpatrick, a civil servant secretly working for the British Resistance, is half Irish and has 'an Irish look'.[30] The Irish war of independence is being replayed as the English war of independence against the European invader.

This is, in both senses, quite a seizure. Opposition to Irish independence, even in the anodyne form of Home Rule, is utterly constitutive of modern British conservatism. The full name of the Tory Party is the Conservative and Unionist Party. The unused appendage may now have some resonance in relation to Scottish nationalism, but its origin was in the struggle against Irish efforts to break up the union. This is in the DNA of Toryism: the creation of an independent Ireland was the work of wreckers and fanatics. And now what is the model to which Brexit Britain must look? – the creation of the Irish Free State, which came into being in 1922.

One of the most remarkable features of the Leave campaigns in 2016 was their absolute refusal to countenance any discussion of Ireland. This would become a classic case of the return of the repressed: Ireland would be the step on which the whole Brexit project would stumble. Some of this repression was down to blithe ignorance. To the extent that the Brexiteers thought at all about Ireland, it was to suggest that any problems with the Irish border could be solved by the obvious solution of Ireland rejoining the UK. Nigel Lawson, chairman of the Leave campaign, suggested before the referendum, 'I would be very happy if the Republic of Ireland – I don't think it's going to happen – were to say we made a mistake in getting independence in 1922, and come back within the United Kingdom. That would be great.'[31]

But in a deeper sense, Ireland did not have to be thought of as a separate problem at all because, post-Brexit, England would *be* Ireland. As reality gradually took hold in 2018, the less extreme Brexiteers began to imagine that it would be better for Britain to *be* the Irish Free State. The idea began to surface in Tory circles that it might be okay to accept a circumscribed Brexit and then gradually expand it in the coming decades because this is what the Irish had done after 1922. The pro-Brexit Conservative MEP Daniel Hannan directly compared Theresa May's Chequers proposals of June 2018 to the approach of the pro-Treaty side in the early years of Irish independence:

> When the Irish Free State left the UK, in 1921, there were all sorts of conditions about Treaty ports and oaths of supremacy and residual fiscal payments. And what very quickly became apparent was not just that those things were unenforceable once the split had been realised; it was that everyone in Britain kind of lost interest in enforcing them. And although there were some difficulties along the way in the 1920s, it turned out to have been better to have grabbed what looked like an imperfect independence and then built on it rather than risking the entire process.[32]

In this vertiginous analogy, in the 1920s and 1930s Britain is the EU and Ireland is, um, Britain. Now, in the post-referendum scenario, the EU is Britain and Britain is Ireland. When the room stops spinning and vision is restored, what can be focused on is the breathtaking nature of the shift in self-image. The

British are now the people against whom they themselves once unleashed Oliver Cromwell and the Black and Tans, the gallant indigenous occupants of a conquered and colonized territory rising up, albeit as Nigel Farage boasted, without firing a shot, against their imperial overlords.

For those of us who are Irish it is tempting to take this as a compliment, but it has one minor flaw. Britain was not colonized by the European Union. By no stretch of the imagination – and the elasticity of the Brexit imagination is astonishing – can the relationship between Brussels and London be credibly construed as being similar to anything that occurred in colonial times between London and Dublin, let alone that between London and Delhi or Nairobi. This is Scott-of-the-*Azamara-Quest* stuff, a hyperbolic inflation of minor inconvenience into epic suffering. As with the Nazi occupation of England, the EU is here playing a pre-scripted role. England needs to think of itself self-pityingly as a colony – therefore it must have a colonizer. If it has been seduced into playing Submissive, somebody has to be playing Dominant.

This has its comic side, but it also has a nasty logic. If there is on the one hand a need to think of oneself as being invaded and colonized and on the other hand no tangible enemy to fulfil this need, the job has to be given to somebody more visibly present. Who is doing the invading? It is the tens of millions of Turks, Iraqis and Syrians who are, in the mendacious pro-Brexit ads, about to head straight for Britain after the imminent accession of Turkey to the EU. Who is doing the colonizing? Those Poles who moved in up the street. What has been transferred once – the guilt of Empire – is free to be transferred again. The old empire appropriates the pain of the subject peoples and then transfers the guilt of invasion and colonization to the immigrant.

It was always possible, in some dark corners of the English imagination, to link 'the Dunkirk spirit', via fears and fantasies of 'invasion', to hatred of the black people who were 'colonizing' the mother country. As the writer of one of the 110,000 supportive letters Enoch Powell received in the fortnight after his 'rivers of blood' speech of April 1968 fulminated: 'I never saw 1 coloured person at Dunkirk and they want to come here and run our little Island what was peaceful and now it is full of MONGREL'S [sic]... I hope you could bring up some of these points in Parliament and better still bring back our FREE SPEECH FOR THE BRITISHER, I MEAN WHITE, AND FREEDOM WHICH WE FOUGHT FOR AT DUNKIRK...'[33] Dunkirk was being replayed as a metaphor for white withdrawal from the threat of a multi-cultural society. As Camilla Schofield has put it, 'The war, and particularly the potent myth of British self-reliance at Dunkirk, served as a means to define who belonged.'[34] And this in turn fed a profound connection between the war and a sense of victimhood. A typical letter to Powell said, 'I'm sure that our boys who died from 1939–1945 to preserve our wonderful country... would turn in their graves if they could see the hordes of invaders we are now getting.'[35]

The quisling theme was also endemic in the revolt against black and Asian migrants. Immigration was proof that a treacherous elite was selling out the victory of the war. 'The white working class are redrawn,' as Schofield writes, 'as victims of a traitorous state... This was, he insisted, an invasion not unlike that which was threatened in 1940.'[36] In Powell's 'rivers of blood' speech, 'The British people who had fought to protect the nation from a German invasion now faced what Lord Elton had just a few years before called an "unarmed invasion".'[37] Powell in the speech quoted an alleged correspondent: 'Never in history, she noted, had any but a "conquered people" been settled by such great numbers of aliens.' It is not hard to see how this strange fusion helps to underpin the mood of Brexit, putting together, as it does, a visceral fear of immigrants with the idea of a heroic retreat from Europe.

'Invasion' is thus a structure of feeling that unites the two great neuroses – encompassing the unfinished psychic business of *both* the Second World War *and* the end of Empire. Anti-immigration sentiment was originally aimed primarily at Afro-Caribbean and South Asian migrants. In the reactionary imagination they embodied not just the end of Empire but the nightmare of reverse colonization, of the Empire striking back by occupying England's own streets. These unarmed invaders can be compared to the Nazis who in turn can be compared to the EU, which is equally a form of unarmed invasion. This metaphor does crucial work for Brexit: it fuses the war, the end of Empire, immigration and the EU into a single image.

Yet there is a final twist. Just as the dark fantasy of fighting the Nazis all over again produced a half reality of planning for wartime conditions after Brexit, the hallucination of being a colony ends up with the terror that post-Brexit Britain will actually *be* a colony. Having talked themselves into the wildly exaggerated notion of Britain as a satrapy of Berlin or a subservient satellite of Brussels, it dawns on the Brexiteers that they are actually creating the very monster they conjured from the depths of the post-imperial imagination. A pre-Brexit Britain cannot reasonably be imagined as a colony, but a post-Brexit Britain can.

The Brexiteers, like some amateurish necromancer, end up recoiling in horror from the spectre they themselves summoned. 'It is impossible to get any bespoke trade deal in two years or so. And for all that time, the UK would be an EU colony – forced to accept our laws with no say,' an EU parliament official tells the British press in 2017.[38] 'Jacob Rees-Mogg: UK must not be EU "colony" after Brexit' blazons the BBC website in December 2017.[39] 'Leaving the EU while remaining in the customs union,' tweets Daniel Hannan in May 2018, 'would be far worse than staying where we are. We'd be an EU colony, subject to taxation without representation.'[40] 'In that respect,' writes Boris Johnson to Theresa May in his letter of resignation as foreign secretary, 'we are truly headed for the status of colony – and many will struggle to see the economic or political advantages of that particular arrangement.' When that happens, of course, there will be one last resort: Brexit was not a heroic failure, it was a marvellous success because we always loved the colonies so much that we wanted to be one.

In 2004, on the 150th anniversary of the charge at Balaclava, the *Daily Express* ran a two-page spread with the glorious headline 'Triumph of the Light Brigade'. It reported that Terry Brighton, curator of the Queen's Royal Lancers regimental museum – descendants of the 17th Lancers who were in the vanguard of the charge – 'rejects the notion that the charge was a failure. Instead he says that it was an amazing success':

'The brigade advanced down the valley in perfect formation despite being fired on by cannons to the front and on all sides,' he said. 'Many saw comrades to the right and left fall from the saddle and were splattered with the blood of horribly shattered men. Yet they not only reached the Russian guns and took a terrible revenge on the Cossack gunners, they then pursued the Russian cavalry behind the guns. This was not a charge that failed.'[41]

In 150 years' time the same, no doubt, will be written of the amazing success of Brexit.

4.

A PINT OF BEER, A PACKET OF PRAWN COCKTAIL FLAVOUR CRISPS AND TWO OUNCES OF DOG SHIT, PLEASE

The clever man who cries
The catch cries of the clown

—W. B. YEATS

In *Fifty Shades of Grey*, the Dominant is a food Nazi. A key clause in the contract Christian seduces Anastasia into signing concerns the most important things she will have to put in her mouth: 'The Submissive will eat regularly to maintain her health and well-being from a prescribed list of foods. (Appendix 4) The Submissive will not snack between meals, with the exception of fruit.' And the most erotic moment in the book – perhaps the only erotic moment – is when Anastasia breaks free of this specific oppression. Nipple clamps are all very well but having to eat for 'health and well-being' is where the bondage must stop. Part of the genius of the anti-European narrative that fed Brexit is that it took all the large anxieties about the unfinished war and the ghosts of Empire and the need to be oppressed and concentrated them on objects of consumption. It used food and drink to make these anxieties not tangible but edible and potable. If Brexit were a play, it would be Samuel Beckett's *Not I*: all mouth.

In 2001, Boris Johnson, then editor of the *Spectator*, was seeking to launch his political career by being adopted as Tory candidate for the safe seat of Henley-on-Thames, Oxfordshire. The selection convention was held in the village hall in Benson, where the presence of the members of the South Oxfordshire Conservative Association was made known by 'the bonnet-to-bonnet array of shiny Jags and Mercs' parked outside.[1] Johnson wooed them with a homily about toast. His wife Marina, he said, had given birth to one of their children in a National Health Service hospital. The staff had brought her toast but while she slept Boris had scoffed the lot.

> And your wife wakes up and says, I say, what happened to that toast? And you say I'm afraid it's no longer with us, or not directly with us ha ha ha; and your wife says, Well what's the point of you? Why don't you go out and hunt stroke gather some more toast as your forefathers did in the olden days? And you go into the highways and byways of the maternity hospital, and I tell you, Mr Chairman, there are babies popping out all over the place; and then you find the person who is i/c toast, and you ask for some more,

and there isn't any more of course, Mr Chairman, because you have had your ration, and when you move to open your wallet, you find that this is no good either. You can't pay for things on the NHS. It's a universal service free at the point of delivery, delivery being the operative word Mr Chairman, ha ha ha. And the whole point of the saga is that it ought to be possible for a well-heeled journalist, who has been so improvident as to eat his wife's toast in the middle of the night, to pay for some more... And this is not as trivial as it sounds, because we need to think about new ways of getting private money into the NHS.[2]

This speech sufficiently impressed the members of the South Oxfordshire Conservative Association that they chose Johnson as a worthy successor to their retiring MP, Michael Heseltine, one of the finest political rhetoricians of his time. But though it may not be in the great tradition of Edmund Burke, it is nonetheless worthy of attention for it contains many of the seeds of Brexit. First, there is the naughty-boy roguish charm. It is a (slightly) grown-up version of a *Just William* story, where instead of stealing a cake at the vicar's tea party, Boris is wolfing his wife's toast. It is disarmingly childish. It functions as an English version of the famous Stanford marshmallow test in which children's capacity for delayed gratification was assessed by offering them a choice between one treat now or two treats a little later. Boris fails the toast test – even his wife's suffering in childbirth is not enough to make him prioritize her needs over his own. Yet even while confessing his sin, he is also evoking the thrills of rebelling against constraint. The none too subliminal message is: screw deferred gratification.

Secondly, the story contains a parable of British politics over the previous half-century. The 'person who is i/c [in charge of] toast' is a parody of the officiousness of a wartime economy and of nationalized industry. Johnson evokes the rationing of food and other necessities that characterized post-war austerity in Britain: 'you have had your ration'. This austere egalitarian-ism ought to have been banished by the Thatcherite market revolution. But the rights of the wealthy are being denied: it ought to be possible for a well-heeled journalist to open his wallet and command the anonymous minion to obey the laws of supply and demand. Only the hangover of socialistic regulation stands in the way of our hero's attainment of his goal of more toast. We almost forget – as we are meant to – that the blame for poor Marina's famishment lies, not with toast-withholding socialism but with the selfish oaf who ate her bread.

Equally, the story epitomizes Johnson's talent for combin-ing comic deflation with political inflation. On the one side, it is self-consciously bathetic. It is, as the wife's sardonic remarks make clear, a parody of the classic quest narrative. Boris must go hunting as his forefathers did in the olden days. He is a bumbling Argonaut in search of the golden bread, an erring knight errant whose holy grail is the Mother's Pride that he himself has snatched from the new mother. Yet on the other side, this parable is also an exercise in political hyperinflation. It really is 'as trivial as it sounds'. Nothing has actually happened other than a fat, greedy man stealing the food meant for his poor post-partum wife. But from it Johnson draws for his audience a huge conclusion: the NHS must be in part privatized.

This is the essential method of what we might call Brexit camp. Johnson's awful puns hardly qualify as Wildean, but we see here the political application of Oscar Wilde's dictum 'That we should treat all trivial things very seriously, and all the serious things of life with sincere and studied triviality.' This will become, in essence, the methodology of Brexit. It will triumph by teaching the English to take trivial things – the petty annoyances of regulation – very seriously indeed, and to regard the serious things – jobs, communities, lives – with sincere and studied triviality.

'Camp,' wrote Susan Sontag, 'is art that proposes itself seriously, but cannot be taken altogether seriously because it is "too much".' But in the camp politics of Brexit, we will come to see a kind of reversal of this procedure: a politics that proposes itself trivially but that has to be taken seriously because its consequences are 'too much'. Johnson's toast tale – like so many of his stories about the European Union – conforms precisely to Sontag's definition of camp as 'the love of the exaggerated, the "off", of things-being-what-they-are-not'. It is openly theatrical: the layers of self-parody and mock-heroic bathos are not hidden – they are part of the performance. But it propels these campy exaggerations into the realms of public policy. Sontag maintained that 'the Camp sensibility is disengaged, depoliticised – or at least apolitical'. But Johnson's genius – and that of the other great Brexit camper Jacob Rees-Mogg – is to make this very disengagement a form of engagement, to make depoliticization a political cause. Once 'politics' is made to mean 'the European Union', an 'anti-political' pose can become politically explosive. The camp style of 'things-being-what-they-are-not' will be turned into a kind of supercharged negation of evidence, of facts, of reality, of consequences.

There were precedents on the Tory right, not least in the ghostly figure who hovers unacknowledged over Brexit, Enoch Powell. Powell's weirdly arch manner and authorship of bad homoerotic poetry gave a strange, knowing theatricality even to his inflammatory racism. The cultural historian Bill Schwarz, who conducted extensive interviews with Powell, says of him

> Powell was a man of studied eccentricity. When shortly after the war his faith in the supreme authority of the empire buckled, he nonetheless retained a feverish hold on his colonial instincts and sensibilities. He laboured hard to maintain his military bearing, his dress and his elaborate diction. When he gravitated toward the Conservative Party his coiffure shifted from severe post-punk to matinée quiff. For all the evident admiration of his own power to reason, the calculated performance (as we would call it these days) of his own selfhood was both knowing and arch. In his very darkness there was bred a highly tuned narcissism... He embraced theatricality, often deployed to wrong-foot his adversaries. His liking for the Marx Brothers should come as no surprise. Inside this dedicated totem to the old order there existed a contrary current: something knowingly impish, or unexpectedly camp, in his presentation of self.

Consider a single word: piccaninnies. When Boris Johnson wrote in 2008 of the Queen, on her visits to Commonwealth countries, being greeted by 'flag-waving piccaninnies' with 'watermelon smiles'[3] he was (surely consciously) echoing Powell's 'rivers of blood' diatribe, delivered forty years previously, which used the same curiously coy Christy Minstrels term of racist abuse. Powell had spoken of the plight of another elderly English lady: 'When she goes to the shops, she is followed by children, charming, wide-grinning piccaninnies.'[4] The word itself configures racism as an archaic, old-world, baroque diminutive, as if it is being uttered, not by a contemporary English politician but by a Southern belle in an old plantation novel.

Equally, in a 1996 think-piece considering the possibility that Britain might leave the EU, Michael Gove evokes the idea that English nationalism can be seen as an oppressed subculture analogous to that of homosexuality before Gay Liberation: 'attachment to the independent nation state now being the love that dare not speak its name'.[5] The words 'the love that dare not speak its name' come from a poem by Alfred Douglas and were notoriously used against Oscar Wilde in his trial for gross indecency: 'What is the love that dare not speak its name?' Here again, we see the urge of those within a privileged Tory elite to take on the mantle of oppression. But more specifically, we see the appropriation of a camp style of discourse that was developed by an abused minority as a form of self-defence.

In this, the roots of Brexit are not in classic reactionary discourse. In general, the far-right doesn't do irony. Its standard pose is of the utmost seriousness: everything is going to hell and only we (or more usually only I, the strongman) can save it. But this is not the pose of the decadent ruling class whose modes of discourse would shape Brexit's politics of magnified grievance. Patrick Melrose in Edward St Aubyn's dissection of that class finds himself 'desperate to escape the self-subversion of irony and say what he really meant, but really meaning what only irony could convey'.[6] What only irony could convey is the huge gap between a statement (I ate my wife's toast and could not get more) and the meaning it is supposed to bear (the NHS must be privatized). Johnson is not using a joke to make a point: the point *is* a joke. Comedy exists in the hiatus between statement and meaning, and this gap is the centre of this whole way of speaking. Johnson is not a politician who is humorous – the humour, however laboured, *is* the politics. 'Ha ha ha' is literally written into his script.

'This is not as trivial as it sounds' will, over time, become perhaps the quintessential Brexit claim. It is the key to a meta-politics of exaggerated grievance. It comments on itself – we all know, don't we, that this story sounds silly? But then it pivots into apparent seriousness: it sounds silly but it is deadly serious. It is beautifully slippery – a grievance may not be as trivial as it sounds while still being very trivial indeed. It is the springboard for a giant leap between the microcosm and the macrocosm – between the toast and privatizing the NHS, between a petty EU consumer regulation and the need to leave the EU. The trivial becomes exemplary, the banal becomes epic.

The last thing to note about this speech that launched

Johnson's political career is the most obvious: it is about food. At the heart of the most effective anti-EU stories is oral gratification – and those who would deny it. Brexit's mythologies are all mouth and stomach. The appeal is literally visceral: They are trying to stop you consuming what you want to consume. And – of course – this is not as trivial as it sounds. You are what you eat (and drink), so by interfering with your right to consume, They are interfering with what you are. Identity is at stake. William Blake might have invited the English to see the world in a grain of sand, but Boris Johnson could invite them to see Englishness in a packet of prawn cocktail flavour crisps.

Perhaps in this he was instinctively touching a raw nerve. One genuinely distinctive aspect of Englishness had long been a decidedly uncontinental taste in food. George Orwell, trying to explain the English character in 1944, wrote, 'The difference in habits, and especially in food and language, makes it very hard for English working people to get on with foreigners. Their diet differs a great deal from that of any European nation, and they are extremely conservative about it. As a rule, they will refuse even to sample a foreign dish. They regard such things as garlic and olive oil with disgust, life is unliveable to them unless they have tea and puddings.'[7]

The great Marxist historian of England, E. P. Thompson, writing in the *Sunday Times* in the run-up to the 1975 referendum, gave this disgust an explicitly anti-Common Market turn, brilliantly fusing English puritanism with anti-capitalist politics: 'It is about the belly. A market is about consumption. The Common Market is conceived of as a distended stomach: a large organ with various traps, digestive chambers and fiscal acids, assimilating a rich diet of consumer goods... This Euro-stomach is the logical extension of the existing eating-out habits of Oxford and North London.'[8]

But by the time Boris Johnson was wooing Oxfordshire's Tories, the eating-out habits of Oxford had lost their ability to function as a marker of unEnglish self-indulgence. English tastes had changed radically, in particular because of Spanish holidays and EU membership. This change, however, left a vacuum for Johnson to fill, an inherited notion of dietary distinctiveness whose very lack of reality made it open to pure invention. The English could be persuaded that 'life is unliveable to them' without prawn cocktail flavour crisps.

There was a precedent. In 1973, there was what a *Daily Mirror* headline called the 'Eurobeer Menace': 'A Common Market threat to British beer united Labour and Tory MPs yesterday. The threat came in reports of a plan by Market authorities to "harmonise" brewing methods.' The Tory MP Sir Gerald Nabarro was quoted as saying, 'This would be a disaster. Our beer is world famous for its strength, nutritional value and excellence.'[9] (In truth, it was world-famous at the time for being piss-poor.) In 1975, when the referendum on membership was approaching, the *Mirror* felt it necessary to reassure readers that such harmonization would be optional and that 'You will still be able to drink a British pint and eat a British loaf.'[10]

But Harold Wilson nevertheless discovered that he could use the fear of Europeans interfering with the British diet to score phoney 'victories'. While the British had accepted decimalization without too much fuss, he played up anxieties that metrication of British imperial measures would be a step too far because it would mean that a pint or a loaf of bread would be different if they were measured in litres or kilos. Returning from a summit in Paris three months after the referendum, Wilson 'proudly announced that he has saved Britain from the horrors of the "Euroloaf" and "Eurobeer". "An imperial pint is good enough for me and for the British people, and we want it to stay that way."'[11] Wilson undoubtedly knew that this was nonsense, but he also knew, as Johnson would discover, that it was the kind of nonsense that sold well. The British had an insatiable appetite for every kind of Euro-menace to their food and drink.

It is not accidental that the metaphor that shaped official Brexit strategy after the referendum of June 2016 was drawn from the unrestrained consumption of food. In November 2016, a Downing Street aide, Julia Dockerill, was photographed emerging from a Brexit strategy meeting with a handwritten memo that included the note: 'What's the model? Have cake and eat it.'[12] This picked up on Boris Johnson's interview with the *Sun* a month earlier in which he suggested 'Our policy is having our cake and eating it. We are Pro-secco but by no means anti-pasto.'[13] This itself picked up on lines Johnson had been using long before the Brexit campaign: 'My policy on cake is pro having it and pro eating it' went back to at least 2014[14] and the prosecco/antipasto joke was first used in a *Daily Telegraph* column in 2008.

But it actually goes back all the way to 1974, the year after Britain joined the Common Market. According to Boris's father Stanley, the joke was his:

We were having a family holiday in a house near Gaiole in Chianti, in the summer of 1974. My mother was staying with us too. I had an old Super 8 camera and I took a film of us having lunch on the terrace, looking out over the Tuscan Hills… 'Here we are!' I say, with my eye to the camera's view-finder. 'Look at this groaning board. A typical Italian peasant feast. Granny Butter is just having a crack at the pasta. Pass Granny the wine, someone!' Pan to audience. 'I'm definitely *pro*-secco but a bit *anti*-pasto.'[15]

Apart altogether from Boris stealing his father's jokes with the same abandon with which he stole his wife's toast, the genealogy of this pun is telling. It is a product both of class privilege and of upper-class Europhilia. In 1974, readers of the *Sun* may have been flocking to Spain for their holidays, but they were not anxious to consume 'a typical Spanish peasant feast'. On the contrary, they had made it clear that they would not consume foreign muck. They had forced the locals to learn that English people would eat only proper English food. As Richard Weight recounts in his fine history of post-war British identity, *Patriots*, 'Once abroad, most Britons disdained foreign food. Ruby Webster, a devotee of Majorca, remembers: "I loved the Spanish people, they were so friendly, but I didn't go much on the food. So I said to the waiter 'have you ever heard of rice pudding?' he said 'no, no, no, not rice in the pudding?' and I said 'yes, yes, yes.' So he took me into the kitchens and I told them how to make it. We had rice pudding every day after that and the English people loved it… because in Majorca they didn't know a lot about English cooking in those days."'[16]

This indeed was one of the great lines of class division. Most *Sun* readers in the 1970s would have been horrified at the notion that they should eat European peasant food. But the privileged classes like the Johnsons could put physical distance between themselves and their compatriots by preferring Chiantishire to Majorca and by savouring the foreign muck that the lower orders disdained. So how could Boris Johnson use his father's joke about prosecco and antipasto in the *Sun* in 2016 without risking his reputation for having the common touch? Precisely because four decades of membership of the European Union had profoundly changed English working-class taste. Italian peasant food hardly seemed foreign any more.

This Europeanization of English taste ought to have made it impossible to deploy fears of foreignness in food and drink as an anti-European trope. But those fears were in fact successfully manipulated – partly because they go very deep and partly because they were cleverly reshaped, not as a story about consumption but as a tale of interference with consumption. Most brilliantly, a long-standing idea that foreign food might be unhealthy was turned into its opposite: an insistence on the right of every English man, woman and child to eat as much crap as he or she chooses.

It is telling that Boris Johnson chose to define himself against the great popular champion in England of precisely the kind of Italian peasant cooking his own family had scarfed from the groaning board on its Tuscan terrace: Jamie Oliver. In 2006, Oliver was leading, through his TV show, *Jamie's School Dinners*, a high-profile campaign to replace processed fare like Turkey Twizzlers with actual food in school meals. The then

Tory leader, David Cameron, praised Oliver to the skies at the party's annual conference in October 2006. But Johnson attacked him, and came to the defence of mothers who had been reported as passing fast food to their darlings through school railings to help them avoid the plague of healthy eating: 'If I was in charge I would get rid of Jamie Oliver and tell people to eat what they like... I say let people eat what they like. Why shouldn't they push pies through the railings?... I would ban sweets from school – but this pressure to bring in healthy food is too much.'[17]

Pushing greasy pies through the school railings becomes an image of English freedom, just as Cordelia Gummer's BSE burger had been in the 1990s. Oliver had pointed out that Turkey Twizzlers contained 34 per cent turkey and were bulked up with water, pork fat, sugar, rusk, tomato powder, wheat starch, dextrose, salt, wheat flour, potassium chloride, hydrogenated vegetable oil, citric acid, spices, onion powder, malt extract, smoke flavourings, garlic powder, colours E160c and E162, mustard flour, sweetener [E951], spice extracts, herb extracts, vegetable oil, turkey skin, salt, wheat flour, dextrose, stabilizer E450, mustard, yeast extract, and the antioxidants E304, E307, E330, E300. But the right to consume E numbers had long been one of Johnson's causes. And, crucially, he had linked it in the public mind with the oppressive nature of the EU. The E stood for Euroscepticism.

In the annals of Brexit, we must not neglect the part played by the prawn cocktail flavour crisp. In April 1991, *The Times* reported that 'Britain's heritage of multi-flavoured potato crisps is threatened by the refusal of the European commissioner for industry Martin Bangemann to countenance changes to an EC directive restricting the use of artificial sweeteners in foods'. The cranky Tory MP Teddy Taylor was quoted in the story: 'What is the point of voting at elections when the decisions that affect your life are made by some bloke in Brussels...'[18] The *Daily Mail* carried an editorial comment under the title 'The nasty taste of Brussels directives': 'Der crunch is coming for munchers of the more exotic-flavoured of crisps... Our own food minister David Maclean yesterday came out in robust opposition to this latest attempt by the Eurocrats to decide for us precisely what we should and should not be allowed to eat. Good for him.'[19]

The inflation of language is striking. Exotic flavours of crisps are suddenly part of 'Britain's heritage', on a par with Stonehenge, Shakespeare and the six wives of Henry VIII. The German nationality of the commissioner Martin Bangemann allows the story to become another episode of Anglo-German conflict ('der crunch') – like two world wars. And in Taylor's rent-a-quote comment, there is a double act of hyping. A packet of crisps becomes a thing that 'affects your life', and the alleged assault on the right to produce and consume it in strange varieties is the demolition of democracy. There is no point in voting at all because some bloke in Brussels will just decide what you can and cannot eat. This may sound trivial but...

In fact, Brussels never banned exotic flavoured crisps – it merely moved to limit the amounts of artificial sweeteners in food that pretended to be made of things like potatoes and vegetable oil. But Johnson, then Brussels correspondent of the *Telegraph*, spotted the opportunity for a patriotic crusade.

What distinguished him from other opportunistic headline-hunters, though, was a genius for simplification. The others picked up on complaints from the British crisp manufacturers that limiting the use of artificial sweeteners would interfere with their right to lavish E numbers on growing children. But while they wrote about the threat to 'multi-flavoured potato crisps', Johnson picked on a single flavour: prawn cocktail.

This showed an intuitive brilliance. In the 1980s, as in the previous two decades, the favourite English three-course meal for dining out on a special occasion was prawn cocktail, steak garni with chips and Black Forest gâteau. Simon Hopkinson and Lindsay Bareham called their book on the English dining experience of that era *The Prawn Cocktail Years*. For reasons that may puzzle anthropologists long into the future, the prawn cocktail – a few (hopefully unfrozen) crustaceans placed in a glass on a bed of shredded lettuce, smothered in a pink Marie Rose sauce and sprinkled with paprika had become the quint-essential English idea of fine dining. But by 1991, it was also becoming an object of snobbish scorn. It was the perfect dish for national neurosis – on the one hand an English version of Proust's madeleine, opening the sensory pathways to memor-ies of first dates and special occasions; on the other, a site of sensitivity about class, sophistication and naffness.

It would have been too lavish a gift to Johnson had the EU actually attempted to ban the prawn cocktail. But his invent-iveness led him to the next best thing – the Brussels war on the prawn cocktail flavour crisp. As he confessed in 2002, 'Some of my most joyous hours have been spent in a state of semi-incoherence, composing foam-flecked hymns of hate to the latest Euro-infamy: the ban on the prawn cocktail flavour crisp.'[20] The fact that there was no ban on the prawn cocktail flavour crisp (it is still freely available over the counter) was no impediment to the foam-flecked hymns of hate. On the contrary, being pure fiction made the story beautifully elastic. Like the tale of Marina's toast, this tiny seed of grievance could blossom into a monstrous oppression.

Just as the simple, ordinary toast could be buttered with an anti-NHS message, Johnson's crisps were salted with an anti-EU appeal to market freedom. Imagining a crisp company executive, he wrote that such a man knows of the Tories 'that we are a capitalist party that will help him sell as much deep-fried potato as he likes... we will die in the last ditch to preserve the prawn cocktail flavour crisp... we don't like too much regulation and will try to preserve his emulsifiers and anti-oxidants.'[21]

But while this may appeal to crisp company executives, the ultra-free market ideology has limited appeal to ordinary voters. The story works only if it can be hyped up even further into the politics of self-pity. It has to become, not mere proof that the 'capitalist party' will do anything its corporate donors want, but a struggle for Englishness itself. Ludicrous as the parable is, it perfectly captures the way Brussels-bashing could be the arena in which an extreme pro-business ideology could be infused with the heady aromas of populist nationalism.

In his diary of his first electoral campaign in 2001, Johnson further magnified the crisp story into a parable of national degradation:

After I had been reporting from Brussels for a couple of years the EU seemed to me, and still does, a repetitive humiliation of British democracy. I remember the tone of voice, when I ran her to earth, of the Brussels bureaucrat who was responsible for drawing up the edict outlawing the prawn cocktail flavour crisp. Someone somewhere had made some mammals eat huge quantities of prawn cocktail flavour crisps, and concluded that they could cause hyperactivity in children. Nonsense, said British health experts. As part of the balanced diet of a British child – two packs Quavers, three chocolate Magnums, 2 oz dog shit a day – the prawn cocktail flavour crisp was thoroughly nutritious. The problem was that British crisps could be sold across the entire single market, and the question was one for qualified majority voting. Britain could be overruled. 'Look', I said to the woman in Directorate-General 5, 'what business is it of yours?' 'It doesn't matter', she snapped back, 'It's not good for children to eat all those crisps.'[22]

There is no reason to suppose that this woman ever existed – Johnson lied all the time about what went on in Brussels. Or that there ever were scientists feeding vast amounts of prawn cocktail flavour crisps to mammals. But they are necessary ingredients of the fable: bossy woman (a little emulsified sexism is also a useful additive to these stories) with an objectionable tone of voice hiding in her bureaucratic lair, plus evil scientists torturing defenceless animals in their lab equals a dark conspiracy to humiliate British democracy, not just once but repeatedly.

The touch of genius, however, is the dog shit. It is what makes the whole exercise so gloriously camp. It is the 'too much' that makes the performance self-aware. Johnson's literal proposition is that prawn cocktail crisps and dog shit have equal rights as parts of the balanced diet of the British child. (Not, of course, the children of people like Johnson himself: the claim simultaneously appeals to the sniggering snobbery of the upper and middle classes – the fat proles eat shit – and to working-class resentment at precisely this kind of sneering.) The implication is that if the interfering bastards in Brussels tried to stop British children being fed dog shit, that too would be a national humiliation and an assault on British democracy. In another context, this would make the whole thing a satire on Euroscepticism itself, a reduction to absurdity of its desperate search for a grievance. But in the campy politics of serious triviality, there is no line between fact and fantasy, between satire and reportage, between the poses of the hero and the clown. When everything is in invisible quotation marks, every-thing has the same level of meaning, whether it is 'British democracy' or '2 oz dog shit a day'.

But we might note a certain historic decline. The high point of British camp came in 1915 when the actor Ernest Thesiger (later to star in the camp classic *The Bride of Frankenstein*) returned from fighting on the Western Front and was asked at a society party what it was like to be a soldier in the Battle of Ypres: 'Oh my dear, the noise! And the people!' (Thesiger also claimed to have tried to join a Scots regiment: 'I thought a kilt would suit me, so I applied at the London Scottish headquar-ters, but my Scottish accent, assumed for the occasion, was apparently not convincing.')[23] This might be called camping down – it takes an apocalyptic reality and reduces it to the level of an unpleasant day trip to the seaside. Johnson's campaign for the prawn cocktail crisp is camping up – it takes a barely existent grievance and inflates it into a political catastrophe. The difference is self-pity: Thesiger (who had a right to it as a wounded veteran) pushes it away; Johnson (who had no right to it as a rich journalist dilettante) seeks it out.

So much, too, for the stiff upper lip. We can see, in this search for slights, the English self-image of stoical resilience dissolving into a quivering super-sensitivity, and hear the clipped tones give way to foam-flecked hymns of outrage. Perhaps this is what happens to a post-imperial ruling class that is no longer taken seriously enough to be attacked and has to go out of its way to be insulted. Edward St Aubyn's Patrick Melrose remembers, 'When I was young… my father used to take us to restaurants. I say "restaurants" in the plural because we never stormed in and out of less than three. Either the menu took too long to arrive, or a waiter struck my father as intolerably stupid, or the wine list disappointed him. I remember he once held a bottle of red wine upside down while the contents gurgled out onto the carpet. "How dare you bring me this filth?" he shouted.'[24]

The twist, though, is that in the anti-EU narrative, the cry is not 'How dare you bring me this filth?' but 'How dare you stop me eating this filth?' And this, too, is a kind of falling-off. It takes a long-established English trope about food and foreignness and turns it back against the English people themselves. In 1998, the Countryside Alliance staged a massive protest in London, largely against plans to ban fox hunting. Some of the protestors held aloft joints of roast beef.[25] They were claiming for themselves a symbol of authentic Englishness and wielding it as a weapon against effete urban elites. There was history behind the gesture: in the mid-eighteenth century, foppish young men whose taste for continental styles were thought to be a threat to English manliness were called 'macaroni' – the eating of pasta instead of roast beef being proof of their perverted foreignness and grounds for suspicion that they harboured unnatural appetites of other kinds.

The Roast Beef of Old England was once an unofficial English national anthem. It began as a verse written by Henry Fielding for *The Grub-Street Opera* in 1731 in which it was sung by the cook-maid Susan, as a protest against the meanness of her mistress:

> When mighty Roast Beef was the Englishman's Food
> It ennobled our Hearts, and enriched our Blood....
> Then, Britons from all nice Dainties refrain
> Which effeminate Italy, France and Spain;
> And mighty roast beef shall command on the Main.

The English right to dine on roast beef was favourably contrasted to the poverty of the French diet and as Protestant defiance of Catholic restrictions on the consumption of meat on holy days and during Lent. But it was also, more practically, a benchmark for unadulterated food. Cooked without additives and served without sauces, it was a guarantee of culinary honesty. In the mad cow wars of the 1990s, the *Daily Express* columnist Ross Benson repeated all of these tropes exactly as if he were writing in the eighteenth century. He boasted that, as an English boy growing up on the continent, he had been mocked as Ross Beef, but took the jibe as being motivated by 'envy at everything British. We are red-blooded, unadulterated and virile. We have no need of the disguise of sauces of the gastronomic or cultural kind. Straightforward and hearty, that's us, just like our beef.'[26]

The absurd twist in the Eurosceptic assault on the regulation of foods by Brussels was that it evoked this centuries-old tradition of using suspicion of foreign meddling in the English diet, but to an opposite purpose. Instead of being a declaration of the English right to plain, honest, unadulterated food, it became a statement of the English right to hidden additives: the E numbers of Old England. The mythic idea of the roast beef of Old England fed a notion that it created and sustained a vigorous, conquering, masculine nation in which even the lower orders would be fit to play their part in world domination. Now, the post-imperial function of the lower orders is to consume and to be consoled. Another of the architects of Brexit, Michael Gove, says poorer people eat fatty food because it gives them 'comfort, solace and pleasure'.[27] Solace for what? For the destruction of their lives by neoliberalism? The thickening of the English body is the market's compensation for the thinning of English working-class hopes. If England cannot fatten itself on the riches of its colonies, its poor must fatten themselves on unregulated junk.

To appreciate the ideology behind this absurdity, we must return for a moment to the Brussels bureaucrat tracked down to her lair by Boris Johnson in his story of the fight to save the prawn cocktail flavour crisp, the ogre who utters that terrible insult to English freedom: 'It's not good for children to eat all those crisps.' It is important that she is a woman, for she is that great English ruling-class archetype, Nanny. She is, in fact, not just Nanny but Supernanny, the embodiment not of the nanny state but of the nanny superstate.

Perhaps the most brilliant linguistic manoeuvre of English neoliberalism was the renaming of the welfare state as the nanny state. The helping hand was transformed at a stroke into a pointing finger. The things that enabled people to be free of drudgery and want were redefined as barriers to their freedom. But this linguistic re-engineering had two related problems. Working-class people didn't have nannies – the image itself might actually remind them of the privileged classes who did. The arch-Brexiteer Jacob Rees-Mogg famously took his nanny out to canvass votes for him, and wrote that 'the British nanny is one of our nation's finest traditions, iconic like a London taxi or a red bus, steeped in history, and, akin to the ravens at the Tower of London, important to the country's wellbeing... They were figures of reassuring authority.'[28] This, of course, is not the desired political image of nanniness, which is that of overweening fussiness rather than tradition-sanctioned and reassuring authority.

The other problem is that many working people rather liked the nanny state. That most English of writers Alan Bennett, who grew up with the welfare state in post-war Leeds, explained in 2009 why he had donated his papers to the Bodleian Library: 'I say proudly that I had a state education, school, university... none of it cost me or my parents a penny. It's a situation which young people in higher education today can only dream of and this is wrong... I see this gift such as it is, as some small recompense both to the University and also, though it is unfashionable to say this, to the state... or the Nanny State as it is disparagingly called. Well, as I say, I was lucky in my time and I'm grateful to have been nannied.'[29]

To survive these challenges, the idea of the nanny state needed to be reinforced in two ways. One was to take it away from its Rees-Moggian connotations and make it somehow defiantly working class. The other was to disguise its real target – free healthcare, public libraries, free universities and other monstrosities – by a process of deflection. It was necessary both to strip out the upper-class connotations of reassuring, motherly authority and to give it a false object. So Rees-Mogg's lovely nanny, redolent of English tradition, becomes Boris Johnson's Brussels ogress scheming to destroy the English 'heritage' of exotically E-numbered crisps. And the rebellion against this nanny superstate is configured as a clarion-call to yobbish face-stuffing: we drink what we like, we smoke what we want, we eat prawn cocktail flavour crisps and we feed our kids Turkey Twizzlers and dog shit – and up yours, Nanny.

In keeping with the camp nature of the whole Brexit discourse, this is a social class drag act. It is striking that the two most crucial figures in the creation of Brexit, Johnson and Nigel Farage, are upper-middle-class men (one a well-heeled columnist, the other a stockbroker turned European political fat cat) posing through oral consumption as lumpen proletarian lads. Johnson dramatized himself in his career-launching toast story as a helpless glutton. He happily confessed that his canvassing efforts in his first campaign as the token Tory

candidate in Clywd South were rendered off-putting to potential voters by his 'habit at every campaign lunch of drinking
a lot of beer, accompanied by very thick-cut cheese and raw
onion sandwiches'.[30]

His Falstaffian girth and championing of cheap junk food
might fool some voters into thinking that he actually dines
on Turkey Twizzlers with a side order of raw emulsifiers and
antioxidants.

Farage, meanwhile, not only champions limitless smoking
but has warned his followers that the World Health Organiza-
tion is 'just another club of "clever people" who want to bully
and tell us what to do. Ignore.'[31] He is constantly photographed
with a pint of beer in his fist. And not just any beer, but Greene
King IPA, of which beer expert Pete Brown notes: 'Loathed
by the trendy craft beer-drinking liberal London media elite, it
was until recently the best-selling cask ale in Britain, the drink
of the common man whom Nigel pretends to be.'[32] The con-
spicuous consumption of unhealthy things is not marginal to
the appeal of Brexit. It is a literal embodiment of rebellion
against the bullies who tell us what to do, the 'clever people'
who think they know better than the real people. Brexit marches
on its distended stomach.

Yet all of this is fundamentally fake. Gove, as the post-2016
minister in charge of British food, notes that 'Helping people
to make better choices in what they eat is fraught territory
politically' – a tiny acknowledgement that the Brexiteers feeding of unregulated and unrestrained consumption of bad stuff
has real-world consequences that have to be faced when you
are in government.[33] The junk food that the Brexiteers made

into a symbol of English freedom translates into an obesity crisis that stirs them into paroxysms of authoritarianism. The anti-nannies become ultra-nannies. Julia Hartley-Brewer, one of the most extreme media boosters of Brexit, admonishes readers of the Brexit-supporting *Daily Telegraph*:

> If you are the parent of a fat child, you are a bad parent. Did everyone get that?... let's stop all this namby-pamby, patronising rubbish about how these parents don't know any better and are just as much victims themselves. They're not victims. They are child abusers.... Demand that the parents come into school to learn how to do the job of parenting properly. And if they refuse, then call in the police and social services and *make* them do it.[34]

This is where a very short journey ends, from the Brussels bureaucrat who thinks children shouldn't eat too many crisps being an intolerable busybody to calling the police on the English parents who let them do so; from embracing childhood obesity as a patriotic cause to condemning it as child abuse; from encouraging the poor to think of consumption as freedom to *make them do it*. Call the police.

But many of those who were persuaded to vote for Brexit as the guarantor of their English rights to put anything they chose into their mouths may have opposing ideas of law and order. Britain feeds itself by importing 40 per cent of its food, and about 10,000 containers of food arrive every day from EU countries. In February 2018, there was a preview of what might happen if the food chains were disrupted by Brexit. Kentucky

Fried Chicken had to shut temporarily half of its 900 branches because of problems with its distributor. There were demands that the police somehow intervene in this crisis. Tower Hamlets Police had to tweet: 'Please do not contact us about the #KFCCrisis – it is not a police matter if your favourite eatery is not serving the menu that you desire.'[35] Likewise police in Manchester pleaded, 'For those who contacted the Police about KFC being out of chicken... please STOP.'[36] But it was, perhaps, too late to stop now. The deprivation of the English right to junk food was clearly a criminal matter.

5.

SADOPOPULISM

> I hurt myself today
> to see if I still feel
>
> —TRENT REZNOR, 'Hurt'

I f you are English and in your fifties or early sixties, two things are likely to be true of you. One is that in 2016 you voted to leave the European Union: 60 per cent of both men and women in the UK aged between fifty and sixty-four did so. The other is that you were, in the immediate period after the UK joined the Common Market, a punk. Or if not an actual punk, then a vicarious one, living off the thrills of the most powerful and original English cultural movement of modern times. These two truths are closely related. At the level of high politics, Brexit may be defined by upper-class twittery. It seems more P. G. Wodehouse than Johnny Rotten. But at the level of popular culture, it is pure punk. John Lydon (formerly Rotten), having initially opposed Brexit, later identified himself with it:

'Well, here it goes, the working class have spoke and I'm one of them and I'm with them.'[1]

In a sense, this is the wrong way round – they are with him, or at least with the Johnny Rotten of the mid-1970s. Had it not had the genius of Take Back Control, a perfect slogan for the Leave campaign would have been Never Mind the Bollocks, Here's Brexit! For it is in punk that we find, not just the nihilistic energy that helped to drive the Brexit impulse but, more to the point, the popularization of masochism. What heroic failure and fantasies of Nazi invasion did for the middle and upper classes, punk did for the young and the working class. Many Brexit voters were formed by its most breathtaking, counter-intuitive stylistic gesture – the idea of masochism as revolt, of bondage as freedom. Punk took bondage gear out of the bedroom and onto the street; Brexit took coterie self-pity out of the media-political boudoir and into real politics.

Objectively, the great mystery of Brexit is the bond it created between working-class revolt on the one side and upper-class self-indulgence on the other. There would seem to be an unbridgeable gulf of style and manner – let alone of actual economic interests – between the stockbroker superciliousness of Nigel Farage or the self-parodic snootiness of Jacob Rees-Mogg on the one side and the raw two-fingered defiance of working-class patriotism on the other. Brexit depended on an ostensibly improbable alliance between Sunderland and Gloucestershire, between hard old steel towns and rolling Cotswold hills, between people with tattooed arms and golf club buffers.

One great binding agent was 'Anarchy in the UK', the sheer

joy of being able to fuck everything up. Boris Johnson, who used The Clash's 'London Calling' as the theme song for his successful campaign to be mayor of London, also chose the same band's version of 'Pressure Drop' on *Desert Island Discs* in October 2005. On that programme, in a rare moment of self-reflection, Johnson spoke of the pleasure of making trouble that motivated his mendacity: 'so everything I wrote from Brussels, I found was sort of chucking these rocks over the garden wall and I listened to this amazing crash from the greenhouse next door over in England as everything I wrote from Brussels was having this amazing, explosive effect on the Tory party, and it really gave me this I suppose rather weird sense of power'.[2]

Essentially, this differs not at all – either as a psychological satisfaction or as a career move – from the way Johnny Rotten made himself famous: 'Johnny Rotten, a member of the group,' the *Guardian* reported in 1976 after the Sex Pistols had exploded into wider British consciousness in an outrageously offensive TV interview, 'said in a BBC interview that he had launched himself to stardom by walking up and down the King's Road in Chelsea, spitting at people. "I did it because they were stupid."'[3]

Throwing rocks over the garden wall to hear the crash from the neighbour's greenhouse windows is the upper-middle-class Home Counties version of spitting at people on the King's Road because they are stupid. And each has the same performative quality of edgy clowning in which everything is at once very funny and highly sinister. The somewhat despairing question that Bill Grundy asked in his notorious Sex Pistols TV interview – 'Are you serious or are you just... trying to make me laugh?'[4] – hangs over Johnson's entire political and journalistic career. Tory anarchism always had a taste for the outrageous: before the Sex Pistols said 'fuck' on television, the last person to do so was Sir Peregrine Worsthorne, then deputy editor of the *Sunday Telegraph* and an obvious journalistic model for Johnson.

They are all bad boys. It is not accidental that the far-right Faragist side of the Brexit movement chose to paint itself as a political wing of the Sex Pistols. Its supplier of dark money, Arron Banks, called his hastily cobbled-together book *The Bad Boys of Brexit: Tales of Mischief, Mayhem & Guerrilla Warfare in the EU Referendum Campaign*. 'Let's shake this up,' Banks records himself saying to Nigel Farage in July 2015 as they are planning what would become an openly racist campaign. 'The more outrageous we are, the more attention we'll get; the more attention we get, the more outrageous we'll be.'[5] In the book's cast list, we get, for example, Chris Bruni-Lowe, described by Banks with admiration as 'Farage's energetic director of strategy and data nerd. Rules the UKIP office through brutal, laddish mockery...'

Mischief, mayhem, bad boys, brutal laddish mockery, the knowledge that the more outrageous they were the more attention they would get – all of this was pioneered by the Sex Pistols' Svengali Malcolm McLaren. It would be a good quiz question to ask whether this passage is by McLaren or Banks: 'I had created a feeling that was both euphoric and hysterical. On that tour bus, you couldn't help but be aware of an enormous range of possibilities – that whatever was happening couldn't be predicted, that it was a movement towards a place unknown. We had the means now to start a revolution of everyday life.'[6] It is actually McLaren on the Pistols' first tour, but it could describe, word for word, the careening course of the Brexit campaign.

Aside from these affinities between Tory anarchism and punk nihilism, there are two deeper ways in which being a punk in the 1970s might have prepared you to be a Leave voter in 2016. One is that punk was actually a brilliant, unexpected and thrilling reinvention from the bottom up of the English cult of heroic failure. McLaren's enterprise was consciously self-destructive: 'My intention was to fail in business, but to fail as brilliantly as possible. And only if I failed in a truly fabulous fashion would I ever have the chance of succeeding.'[7] More importantly, for the young people who actually adopted it, punk was a way of reclaiming dignity by defiantly celebrating their own failure to get on in the approved manner. Its style was the playing up of wretchedness, the creation of fashion from the detritus of consumerism – wearing bin liners and ripped T-shirts, turning the safety pin, shameful emblem of poverty, into a form of decoration. It was the ultimate triumph of failure – and of treating triumph and failure as twin imposters. It is not as far as it seems from the stiff upper lip to the curled lip, from the heroic not caring of Captain Scott to the great snarl of Rotten's 'And we don't care' at the end of 'Pretty Vacant'.

But punk also created the most powerful paradox in the deep neurosis of Brexit: the strange psychic mash-up of revolt and pain, of bondage and freedom, of liberation and self-harm. McLaren and Vivienne Westwood's clothes shop SEX sold 'fetish wear – rubber and leather gear – that would at once appeal to a specialized market and be adopted by teenagers'. The idea, as Westwood explained, 'was to take these taboo garments "out of the bedroom and into the streets: now that would be really revolutionary!"'[8] It was not just clothes – studded wristbands and dog collars were also taken from the S&M clubs onto the streets.

John Lydon also pioneered the idea of the straitjacket as a fashion item: 'The bondage suits that Vivienne made were wonderful, great, crazy things. But they actually came from a photo-shoot I did some time earlier, where I was in a real bondage suit. You know, from the mental asylum. And I liked it. I liked the confinement of it, the restriction.'[9] Lydon described the pleasures of wearing these bondage suits as a kind of self-abnegation: 'You put that on, and basically you're insulting yourself, but you're also clearing yourself of all egotism.'

It is striking that this idea of sadomasochism as 'really revolutionary' dovetailed with the more mainstream dark fantasies of defeat – punk had its own version of the Nazi invasion of England. One of Johnny Rotten's signature Westwood-designed shirts, worn with bondage-style leather gear, has the slogan Destroy, an altered image of a penny postage stamp in which Queen Elizabeth's head is being cut off, and a huge swastika. In Dennis Morris's iconic photograph, Rotten, while wearing this outfit, is posed like Christ on the Cross, the ultimate image of glorious suffering.

Lydon, in retrospect, found it hard to understand what this was about: 'Vivienne Westwood took the style into really dangerous territory, when, for example, she adopted the swastika.

That was a seriously challenging thing to be wearing. I don't have a useful answer as to why it was considered acceptable.'[10] But this was more than just a random assemblage of images. As Jon Savage notes, 'As well as T-shirts sporting gay, S&M and paedophile imagery, SEX sold Nazi memorabilia and arm-bands sporting swastikas.'[11] Punk stormtroopers paraded down the King's Road in genuine Nazi relics.

The English generation that was shaped by punk thus absorbed more than a renewed and radically re-energized idea of heroic failure. It was familiarized with what would otherwise be an outlandish contradiction – the fusion of freedom with self-inflicted pain. Wild revolt is one side of the coin but the other is pleasurable confinement, restriction, bondage. There is in all this both a breaking free and a submission to being tied up. A single sentence of McLaren's says it all: 'These trousers, our bondage trousers, were a declaration of war against repression.'[12] To translate that into bad-boy Brexitese: any transgression is revolutionary even if it celebrates self-harm.

Why do people cut themselves? Obviously, because they are unhappy, frustrated, angry. They feel that no one cares about them, no one listens to them. But it still seems hard to understand the attractions of inflicting pain on yourself. Three things seem to make cutting addictive. One is that it gives the pain you feel a name and a location. It becomes tangible and visible – it has an immediate focus that is somehow more tolerable than the larger, deeper distress. The second is that it provides the illusion of control. You choose to do it – you are taking an action and producing a result. It is a kind of power, even if the only way you can exercise that power is over yourself and even if the only thing you can do to yourself is damage. And the third is that it can seem in an unhappy mind like an act of love. You can hurt yourself *for* someone or something. 'So,' sings the great balladeer of English self-pity Morrissey, 'scratch my name on your arm with a fountain pen / This means you really love me.'[13] For some, marking Leave on the ballot paper in June 2016 was a way of scratching the name of England on their arms to prove their love.

Even though these actions are irrational, the distress that leads to them is often entirely rational. It may be very well-founded. Maybe it's quite true that nobody cares about you. Maybe your parents are so wrapped up in their own conflicts and obsessions that they don't really listen to you or pay attention to what's going on in your life. Maybe you feel powerless because you actually are powerless.

Being angry about the European Union isn't a psychosis – it's a mark of sanity. Indeed, anyone who is not disillusioned with the EU is suffering from delusions. The slow torturing of one of its own member states, Greece, was just the most extreme expression of a desire to blame the debtor countries alone for the great crisis that hit the Eurozone in 2008. Ireland, Portugal and Spain were all objects of the need, especially in Germany, to satisfy a crudely religious imperative that sinners must be severely punished if the virtue of fiscal discipline is to flourish.

A polity that inflicted such pointless suffering on some of its most vulnerable citizens through so-called austerity is morally askew. The EU lost its moral compass when the Berlin Wall fell. Before that, it was in a competition against communism. The generation of Western European leaders that had experienced the chaos of the continent in the 1930s and 1940s were anxious to prove that a market system could be governed in such a way as to create full employment, fair opportunities, decent public services and steady progress towards economic equality. But when the need to compete with alternative ideologies went away after the collapse of the Soviet Union, the EU gradually abandoned its social democratic and Christian Democratic roots.

It also moved away from evidence-based economics – the German-led austerity drive after 2008 was impervious to the realities of its own failure. The social consequences have been shrugged off. Inequality has risen across the continent: the richest seven million people in Europe now have the same amount of wealth as the poorest 662 million people. There are now 123 million people in the EU at risk of poverty – a quarter of the EU population. This has been allowed to happen because the fear of social and political chaos went out of the system. There is a European technocratic elite (especially in unaccountable institutions like the European Central Bank) that has lost its memory. It has forgotten that poverty, inequality, insecurity and a sense of powerlessness have drastic political repercussions. The EU was founded on a kind of constructive pessimism. Behind its drive towards inclusion and equality lay two powerful words: or else. It was an institution that knew that, if things are not held together by a reasonable expectation that life will get better for ordinary people, they will fall apart. In the best sense, the EU itself was a Project Fear. Without that fear, the project became arrogant, complacent and obsessed with grand schemes like the ill-designed euro.

Working-class communities in England, like their counterparts in most of the EU, are absolutely right to feel that they
have been abandoned. Nigel Farage may lie about many things
but he was not lying when he told potential voters that, over
the previous twenty-five years in Britain, there had been 'a
shocking widening of the class system, where the rich have
got a lot richer and the poor are robbed of the opportunity to
attain their best'.[14]

The distress is real. And Brexit gives the pain a name and a
location – immigrants, and Brussels bureaucrats. It counters
their sense of powerlessness with a moment of real power –
Brexit is, after all, a very big thing to do.

But it's still self-harm. For the cynical leaders of the Brexit
campaign, the freedom they desire is the freedom to dismantle
the environmental, social and labour protections that they call
'red tape'. They want to sever the last restraints on the very
market forces that have caused the pain. They offer a jagged
razor of incoherent English nationalism to distressed and
excluded communities and say, 'Go on, cut yourself, it feels
good.' It does feel good. It is exhilarating and empowering.
It makes English hearts beat faster and the blood flow more
quickly – even if it's their own blood that's flowing. But the
crucial twist is that this self-harm is politically bearable only if
someone else is being harmed more. The masochism doesn't
work without a compensatory element of sadism.

Brexit is often explained as populism, but it is driven
more by what Timothy Snyder in *The Road to Unfreedom* calls
'sadopopulism', in which people are willing to inflict pain
on themselves so long as they can believe that, in the same

moment, they are making their enemies hurt more: 'such a voter is changing the currency of politics from achievement to pain, helping a leader of choice create sadopopulism. Such a voter can believe that he or she has chosen who administers their pain, and can fantasise that this leader will hurt enemies still more. [This] converts pain to meaning, and then meaning back into more pain.'[15]

This definition illuminates much of what is going on in Brexit, but it also highlights the project's short-term problems and long-term contradictions. The most obvious short-term problem is the 'leader of choice'. Snyder is thinking of Vladimir Putin, Donald Trump and their various imitators in Europe and elsewhere. Brexit did have a leader of choice – but he was too incompetent to actually effect the transfer of power that this revolutionary moment needed.

It is hard to overstate the degree to which Boris Johnson was the single greatest asset for the Leave side in the referendum. He was personally popular, with an average likability rating in pre-referendum polling of 4.5 on the 0–10 scale compared to 4.2 for Jeremy Corbyn, 3.5 for David Cameron and only 3.2 for Nigel Farage. Andrew Cooper, chief pollster for the Remain campaign, admitted that 'during the referendum campaign it was clear from all our tracking research that Boris was having a big impact. This came through clearly in the focus groups and in our (weekly, twice-weekly, then daily) polling, Boris invariably came top on the question of which politician has made the most persuasive impact…'[16]

More importantly, how people felt about Johnson was a very close predicter of how they would vote in the referendum:

'Feelings about Johnson had very strong effects on the probability of casting a Leave ballot. For voters who really disliked him, the probability of voting Leave was only .09. However, it climbed sharply as people's feelings about Boris became increasingly positive.' For those at the top end of the Boris likability scale, people who gave him a '10 out of 10', the probability of a Leave vote was fully 93 per cent.

But Johnson was entirely unable to live up to expectations expressed by Leave.EU in November 2015 when there were rumours that he might lead the Brexit campaign: 'we would be thrilled to have the support and leadership skills of Boris, who would be a Churchillian figure in the fight to save our country'.[17] This would turn out to be true only in a dystopian *SS-GB*-style thriller in which Britain actually lost the war. Johnson's leadership skills were so outstanding that he could not actually make himself leader of a country that had just effectively voted for him. He came, after all, from a decadent and dilettante political elite for whom, as Edward St Aubyn puts it, 'It was better if a person "could have been" Prime Minister than if he *was* Prime Minister: that would have shown vulgar ambition.'[18]

Johnson had no strategy, no tactics, no serious intent at all. And for a very good reason – Leave was not supposed to win. Johnson told David Cameron when he informed him of his decision to back Brexit that 'he doesn't expect to win, believing Brexit will be "crushed"'. He also had no idea of the actual consequences of leaving the EU. As Cameron reported the phone call to his communications director Craig Oliver: 'He actually said he thought we could leave and still have a seat on the European Council – still making decisions.'[19] (This would be simply unbelievable in any other context, but Johnson, after all, was the author of a book about Churchill which mentioned in passing that the Germans took Stalingrad.) This breathtaking ignorance meant that the English revolution immediately became more like a medieval carnival in which the crowd sweeps up the village idiot and proclaims him as king for the week. Johnson was in fact King Brexit for slightly less than a week, from the morning of the referendum result on 24 June to his ignominious withdrawal from the race to succeed David Cameron as prime minister on 30 June.

Here, too, we see Brexit's extraordinary ability to bring to life its own more ludicrous imaginings. One of these was the hankering for that 'Churchillian figure in the fight to save our country'. For a democracy, Britain had a strange yearning – rooted, like so much else, in the experience of the Second World War – for the unique saviour who can rescue it not just from imminent danger but from moral weakness. Johnson had made himself a high priest of this cult: the subtitle of his 2014 book *The Churchill Factor: How One Man Made History*, said it all. There were none too subtle hints at reincarnation. In Robert Harris's *Fatherland*, after all, Churchill was still alive in Canada – why should not his defiant spirit transmigrate into the only man fit to lead the country in its latest hour of need? As the historian Richard Evans pointed out in his review in the *New Statesman*, the question that hovered over all of Johnson's descriptions of Churchill was 'who is this meant to remind you of?'[20]

But Johnson is no more a reincarnation of Churchill than a packet of prawn cocktail flavour crisps is a token of national enslavement. Of all his ludicrous exaggerations this was the most outlandish. It did, however, contain one important truth: if Johnson was the only great leader who could save the Brexit project, it was inevitably doomed. The manner of his failure may have been spectacularly inept, but in fact Johnson was bound to fail. He embodied a fatal flaw in the Brexit project: the self-pitying grievances that it was designed to address could not in fact be addressed. Why? Because they did not exist. A revolution must cloak itself in an idea of justice: the wrongs done by our oppressors will now be righted. Political prisoners will be freed, exiles returned, land redistributed, collaborators punished, heroes rewarded. But there were no EU dungeons to be thrown open. There were only trivial fictions.

The revolutionary regime that Johnson was supposed to lead could not restore the right to give donkey rides on beaches or bring curved bananas back to the shops or stop dictating the precise size and shape of a Christmas tree or liberate British trawlermen from the ignominy of having to wear hair nets. All of these had been reported in British tabloids as oppressive realities, but they were just vivid stories, nothing more. Above all, prawn cocktail flavour crisps could not be restored to the millions of children craving them for the simple reason that they had never ceased to be available.

The point about the whole Borisovian Brussels-bashing project was that it could survive anything except success. Its great strengths were its apparent tangibility – it took the vast, tedious odyssey of the EU and reduced it to things that people could touch and feel and, more importantly, consume: beer, crisps, bananas – and its campness, the knowing way that these things were hyper-exaggerated into icons of identity. It took Europe down to microcosmic minutiae and then blew them up again into a macrocosmic tale of oppression.

But these very strengths turned against themselves at the moment of 'liberation'. The tangibles crumbled at a touch – they no longer had any political meaning. And the exaggerations were instantly deflated when the context suddenly changed. They only meant anything when they were stones being thrown gleefully over the neighbour's garden wall. The camp, ironic discourse that underpinned Brexit was an in-joke that could not live outside the very thing it sought to subvert: the EU. It was an elaborate form of courtier's humour – it had meaning only while there was a court to mock and fellow courtiers to get the jokes. It worked only when Britain was in Europe – the whole joke was dependent on living a double existence, being part of the Union but pretending to be on the outside, being actually in but imaginatively not *of* the EU. It was a drag act that suddenly had to appear in street clothes.

It is telling that Johnson's mendacity was utterly exposed in a parliamentary Treasury Committee hearing just three months before the Brexit referendum. The questioning by the (Tory) chairman of the committee, Andrew Tyrie, is like watching a kitten bouncing into a combine harvester:

> TYRIE: I would like to turn to your article in the *Telegraph* on 22 February, where you say that there are these ludicrous rules emanating from the EU and that this is a reason for your decision to leave. One of the ludicrous rules that you cite is: 'An EU rule that says you can't recycle a teabag and

that children under eight can't blow up balloons'... Can you tell me which EU regulation or directive says that children under eight cannot blow up balloons?

JOHNSON: Yes, the European Commission's own website. I would be happy to give you the number of the press release in a moment. The European Commission's own website says, 'Adult supervision is required in the case of the use of uninflated balloons by children under eight'. In my household, more or less only children under eight are allowed to blow up balloons, Mr Tyrie. It is absolutely ludicrous to have this kind of prescription set out at a European level. I think it is absolutely bonkers and I think you do too.

TYRIE: What it actually says, Boris – I have the toy safety directive requirements in front of me – is, 'Warning: children under eight can choke or suffocate', and it is asking that this warning be placed on the packaging. It is not requiring or forbidding—

JOHNSON: It is requiring it to be placed on the packaging.

TYRIE: It is requiring a warning to be placed on the packaging. It is not prohibiting children under eight from blowing up balloons.

As for his claims that 'you can't recycle a teabag' under EU law, Johnson had to admit that this was in fact a decision taken by Cardiff City Council and was entirely a matter of local jurisdiction. And his claim that 'There really is European legislation on the weight, dimensions and composition of a coffin' was similarly eviscerated by Tyrie: 'It is not EU

regulation at all, is it? In fact it is a Council of Europe convention on the transfer of corpses. In there, there is no reference
to coffin weight or dimensions, nor is there any EU legislation, nor is the UK a signatory. The story is a figment of your
imagination.'[21]

But the point about this is that it didn't matter at all. At the
most basic level, you cannot expose a naked man: Johnson's
mendacity had never been other than bare-faced and bare-
cheeked. He thrived, not in spite of it, but because of it. When
Johnson left Brussels in 1994, James Landale, who was working
there for *The Times*, composed some verses in his honour, a
pastiche of Hilaire Belloc's Matilda with the *Telegraph*'s foreign
desk in the part of Matilda's aunt:

> Boris told such dreadful lies
> It made one gasp and stretch one's eyes.
> His desk, which from its earliest youth
> Had kept a strict regard for truth,
> Attempted to believe each scoop
> Until they landed in the soup.[22]

'Boris lies' was like Jonathan Swift's 'Celia shits' – a shocking discovery only to those who led the most sheltered of existences.

While the UK was still in the EU, the public exposure of
Johnson's lying was thus a kind of category error. It was exactly
like a man standing up in a theatre and shouting at the actors:
you're lying, Richard III never offered his kingdom for a horse
or Lady Macbeth was a lovely woman. Of course, Boris's facts
were a figment of his imagination because, in a sense, Boris

himself was a figment of the English imagination, a necessary invention. His stories were essentially comic anecdotes of crazed bureaucracy, little sketches in which Boris as John Bull is pursued by dastardly foreign maniacs trying to bind him in red tape, all speeded up in time to the Benny Hill theme tune. They were even rather reassuring – after all, if a supposed rule on the size of our coffins is the worst we have to look forward to, life may not be so bad. We can have the self-pity without the tears.

But once Leave actually won the referendum, this comic universe imploded. Some lies – I am going to ban Muslims and build a wall – can lead to power because they connect, however tenuously, to theoretically possible acts of government. 'An EU rule that says you can't recycle a teabag' connects to nothing. It is like Noam Chomsky's famous example of a sentence that conforms to the structure of a grammatical assertion without being a statement of anything at all: Colourless green ideas sleep furiously. It is not even false – its truth content is zero. And even if it had been true, so what? Does the revolutionary people's government issue a decree that teabags may now be recycled? Does that feel like Independence Day? In Boris's camp performance, every statement came with in-built quotation marks – it was a comedian's catchphrase. But on 23 June 2016, all the quotation marks fell off – this was now supposed to be *about* something. The awful truth was that it simply wasn't.

This matters, not because of the ludicrous personality politics of the Tory Party's succession crisis, but because it exposed the fundamental problem of Brexit as a popular revolt – the problem of taking power. In order – in Snyder's terms –

to convert pain into meaning, there had to be a leader who could compensate for the self-harm inflicted by the people on themselves by inflicting even greater harm on others. Donald Trump, for all his monstrosities, fulfils this need for his working-class supporters – objectively they hurt themselves in voting for him but he actually took power and is serious about inflicting pain on their perceived enemies. Without a transfer of power, Brexit confronts an insoluble problem: who is to inflict the pain and who is to feel it most?

Because it can never supply those answers, Brexit can never create a sustainable meaning from the pain. For at its heart, it replays the old Dublin music hall song: 'We had sham pain that night, and real pain next morning.' It is a release, not from the real anguish of life in deindustrialized communities, but from the phantom agony inflicted by the long campaign to make the English think of themselves as Submissives to the EU's Dominant.

Brexit is a strange hybrid – a genuine national revolution against a phoney oppressor. It has the form of a moment of liberation without the content. The people get out of the Red Room of Pain only to find themselves in the Red White and Blue Room of Pain. All that really changes is that it becomes less clear who is supposed to inflict the agony and who is supposed to suffer it. W. B. Yeats cynically imagined revolution through the image of the beggar on horseback whipping the beggar on foot. The revolution comes, the beggars change places, but the whipping goes on. In Brexit, the whipping certainly goes on, but no one has really changed places. One faction of the Tory Party and its journalistic hinterland lost a game and the other won – there is very little pain for the vanquished and very little real power to inflict it for the victors.

This is why Brexit cleaves so closely to what George Orwell identified as the problem of change in the novels of Charles Dickens: 'It seems that in every attack Dickens makes upon society he is always pointing to a change in spirit rather than a change in structure.'[23] This is why it can, in Orwell's phrase, 'combine such purposelessness with such vitality'.[24]

Even as a game of chance, however, Brexit is especially odd. It is a surreal casino in which the high-rollers are playing for pennies at the blackjack tables while the plebs are stuffing their life savings into the slot machines. For those who can afford risk, there is very little on the table; for those who cannot, entire livelihoods are at stake. The backbench anti-Brexit Tory MP Anna Soubry rose to her feet in the Commons in July 2018, eyed her Brexiteer colleagues and let fly: 'Nobody voted to be poorer, and nobody voted Leave on the basis that somebody with a gold-plated pension and inherited wealth would take their jobs away from them.' But if that's not what people voted for, it is emphatically what they got: if the British army on the Western Front were lions led by donkeys, Brexit is those who feel they have nothing to lose led by those who will lose nothing either way.

One business person tweeted in August 2018 that Jacob Rees-Mogg's company had just sent him a targeted ad on social media offering to "Brexit proof" his investments. But all the main Brexiteers are Brexit-proof. It is not for nothing that some of the leading Brexiteers like Nigel Farage and Rees-Mogg have been shaped by the City of London and the financial industry's culture of risk. Farage in his book, *The Purple Revolution*, confessed, 'I love a gamble, I love stacking up the odds... Not only did trading in the City help whet my appetite for taking a gamble, it taught me how to get out when the trade started to go wrong, and to brush yourself off when the losses started mounting up.' Losses, that is, of other people's money.

Farage also explained why he left the City: 'The fun has gone, compliance officers rule and even as I was preparing to leave the City I was having to fill out such things as "risk assessments". It was just not for me.' Farage fondly recalled an example of this heroic indifference to risk learned while working for the Rousse broking house: 'One morning in the early 1990s, having been working in the City for a decade, I lost a seven-figure sum in the course of a morning on the zinc market. Not a good day, and it was only lunchtime... Contemplating the sobering loss I had just run up, I grabbed my jacket to head out into Broadgate, with the aim of being less sober while I considered how much money I was down. "Where do you think you are going?" my boss yelled. "Out to lunch – but if you want me to take my jacket off again and stay put, I can start losing the same amount this afternoon if you'd rather."'[25]

This is heroic failure with all the heroism removed. It has the indifference, the resignation to suffering, the transformation of a screw-up into a demonstration of character. But the suffering is that of others – some other poor sod is being sent out of the tent into the Antarctic wastes and told to take some time coming back. Brexit is the irruption into politics of the risk culture of the City.

When Farage writes of learning to get out when the trade is going wrong and to brush yourself off when the losses start mounting up, he does not mean having the decency to stop and admit that the project is failing. He means that he and his cohorts can always walk away from the wreckage and pretend that their own survival is at best heroic, at worst cause for a good self-deprecating story over several lunchtime pints. For the working-class voters who were crucial to the Brexit vote, this means that the reality is not so much that they are taking a gamble but rather that they are being gambled *with*. They are the 'other people' in their leaders' gambles with other people's money. Their pain is not and will not be shared by their champions. Who, then, can give it meaning? Who can articulate with authority what sadopopulism must be able to express: this hurts them more than it hurts us?

In the absence of any real risk on the part of Brexit's own leaders, the enemies on whom greater hurt might be inflicted might have seemed obvious enough: the EU and immigrants. But neither of these quite works. The EU certainly stands to suffer from Brexit, but obviously much less than the UK will. Attitudes to immigration are complex and ambiguous: just 31 per cent of Leave voters want a sharp reduction in EU immigration and a big part of the anti-immigration mood flowed from an entirely false belief that hundreds of thousands of EU nationals, especially from Eastern Europe, regarded the UK as a soft touch and arrived as 'welfare tourists'.[26] Precisely because this belief was unfounded, the expectations of those who voted Leave in the belief that all the immigrants would immediately go home were not and cannot be fulfilled. There is here the downside of the mendacity that fuelled Brexit. You can invent enemies, but then you can't hurt these figments. Spectres you have summoned from your own neuroses cannot be made to feel pain because they do not exist.

The only enemy open to punishment was thus the enemy within: those who had voted Remain and their political representatives, parliamentarians insisting on the very parliamentary sovereignty that was supposed to be restored by Brexit, judges exercising their professional functions of scrutiny. Yet here too there are impossible contradictions. On the one hand, the enemy within has to be set against 'the will of the people'. On the other, even to the extent that there is such a thing as 'the people', its will has to be limited to a single, negative act: leaving the EU. The popular will is a one-time offer that expired on 23 June 2016. And to bridge this gap, the Brexiteers had to resort to a peculiar combination of revolutionary and authoritarian rhetoric. They had to present themselves at one and the same time as 'strong and stable' governors and as tribunes of the risen people.

One way of thinking about this dilemma is to consider that most English of upheavals: the bloodless revolution. Leaving aside the awful murder of Jo Cox, the Brexit referendum is the fourth in a series: the restoration of the monarchy in 1660, the replacement of the Stuarts by William of Orange in the Glorious Revolution of 1688 (catastrophically violent in Ireland but largely peaceful in England) and the creation of the welfare state after 1945. These first three each had distinctive characteristics – respectively a restoration of a previous regime and polity, a replacement of a governing elite and a redistribution of resources from elites to the masses. So which of these does Brexit most resemble?

All of them and none of them. It wants to be a restoration – of Britain as a great power, of England as it used to be. But neither of these things is possible. It is a kind of elite transfer of power, but on a completely negligible level. The replacement of James II by William of Orange had very deep consequences that made it far more than just a swapping of kings – it ended the threat of a Catholic monarchy and guaranteed the Protestant identity that would underpin Britishness for centuries. David Cameron being replaced by his own home secretary doesn't have those epic reverberations. It rhetorically hinted at being a recommitment to the welfare state – the infamous claim that £350 million a week would be taken from Brussels and given to the National Health Service and May's first speech on entering Downing Street in which she promised to right the 'burning injustice' of poverty and inequality. But the £350 million was a lie and there was no chance at all that May was going to be the new Clement Attlee.

So the historical models didn't work. The only recourse was to yet another *as if*: to behave as if the bloodless revolution had in fact been bloody. This meant, in a delicious irony, imagining the English revolution *as if* it were the French Revolution. On 18 May 2016, a month before the vote, Nigel Farage told the BBC 'it's legitimate to say that if people feel they have lost control completely – and we have lost control... then violence is the next step'. But in fact the next step in the overthrow of imaginary oppression was imaginary violence. It was another costume drama, in which May and her government pretended to be the Committee of Public Safety, guardians of the people's will against traitors and fifth columnists.

To take power in place of the actual leader of the revolution, Johnson, May had to embrace a literal but entirely phoney populism in which the narrow and ambiguous majority who voted for Brexit under false pretences must be reimagined as 'the people'. But this is not English conservatism – it is pure Jean-Jacques Rousseau: the people express the General Will freely in a majority vote but, once they have done so, dissent is treason. The General Will had been established on that sacred referendum day. And it must not be defied or questioned.

Hence, Theresa May's allies (or should that be masters?) in the *Daily Mail* and the *Daily Express*, using the language of the French revolutionary terror, characterized recalcitrant judges and parliamentarians as 'enemies of the people' and 'saboteurs'. The *Mail*'s 'Enemies of the People: Fury at "out of touch" judges who have declared war on democracy' presented the judiciary as subversives.[27] The accompanying article quoted Nigel Farage's dark warning that 'I now fear that every attempt will be made to block or delay the triggering of Article 50. If this is so, they have no idea of the public anger they will provoke.' Given his earlier warnings of violence, the meaning was clear. If there was a 'war on democracy', the Brexiteers would have to take up arms. As Farage boasted to a cheering audience at Southampton Concorde Club, he would personally 'don khaki, pick up a rifle and head for the front lines'.[28] *Aux armes, citoyens!* With a pint in one hand and an Armalite in the other.

Headlines like 'PM tells the Brexit saboteurs to back off'[29] and 'Saboteurs are doing us down' led naturally to calls for loyalty tests for public servants and the rooting out of those who failed them. Frederick Forsyth in the *Express* made this explicit: 'Those pro-EU fanatics seeking to frustrate the clear public will are almost entirely on the public payroll. My ball-park figure? Eighty per cent – and should be the subject for a huge clear-out. Even if a few hundred received their marching orders, the message to the rest would be very clear. To know that every penny entering your bank account comes from the British taxpayer is a privilege. It is to be repaid with loyalty. Those with a different life-calling can get a job in the private sector and pay for themselves.'[30] He later went the whole hog and labelled anyone within the public service who did not believe that Brexit was a pure triumph a 'traitorous fifth column'.[31] When Thomas Mair, the far-right fanatic who murdered Jo Cox during the referendum campaign, told his trial that his name was 'Death to Traitors, Freedom for Britain', he was at the extreme end of a spectrum that stretched into respectable mainstream opinion. And this rhetoric had been prepared for – it sprang from the long history of imagining an invaded Britain in which it was only right for the government to take hard measures against saboteurs and fifth columnists.

This is why May called a general election in 2017. Her decision to do so – when she had a working majority in Parliament – was not pure vanity. It was the inevitable result of the *völkisch* rhetoric she had adopted when she told her first Tory Party conference as leader that 'if you believe you're a citizen of the world, you're a citizen of nowhere', openly evoking the far-right (and Stalinist) trope of 'rootless cosmopolitans' who did not deserve citizenship.[32]

A working majority is not enough when these concepts are being evoked – in a revolutionary war, the unified people must have a unified Parliament and a single, uncontested leader: one people, one Parliament, one Queen Theresa to stand on the cliffs of Dover and shake her spear of sovereignty at the damn continentals. With the Labour Party then in disarray and its leader deemed unelectable, the polls were putting the Tories twenty points ahead and telling May that her coronation was inevitable. All she had to do was repeat the words 'strong and stable' over and over and Labour would be crushed for ever. The opposition would be reduced to a token smattering of old socialist cranks and self-evidently traitorous Scots. Britain would become in effect a one-party Tory state. An overawed Europe would bow before this display of British staunchness and concede a Brexit deal in which supplies of cake would be infinitely renewed.

The problem was that May wasn't 'the chosen leader' and could not make anyone believe that she was. If you're going to try the *uno duce, una voce* trick, you need a charismatic leader with a strong voice. The Tories tried to build a personality cult around a woman who doesn't have much of a personality. May is a common or garden Home Counties conservative politician. Her stock in trade is prudence, caution and stubbornness. The vicar's daughter was woefully miscast as the Madame Lafarge of the Brexit revolution, the embodiment of the British popular will sending saboteurs to the guillotine. She is awkward, wooden, and, as it turned out, prone to panic and indecision under pressure.

But to be fair to May, her wavering embodied a much

deeper set of contradictions. Those words she repeated so robotically, 'strong and stable', would ring just as hollow in the mouth of any other Conservative politician. This is a party that has plunged its country into an existential crisis because it was too weak to stand up to a minority of nationalist zealots and tabloid press barons. It is as strong as a jellyfish and as stable as a flea. And the idea of a single British people united by the Brexit vote is ludicrous. Not only do Scotland, Northern Ireland and London have large anti-Brexit majorities, but many of those who did vote for Brexit were deeply unhappy about the effects of the Conservative government's austerity policies on healthcare, education and other public services.

So it didn't work. The Committee of Public Safety phase of the Brexit revolution ended less than a year after the referendum when the Tories failed to win a parliamentary majority in the June 2017 general election. May's electoral failure thus marked the larger failure to evoke 'the people' as a single entity and to mobilize it against traitors. In this, the fantasy of inflicting pain on the enemy within also failed. There could be no authoritarian power to punish judges, parliamentarians and dissenters. The problem of converting pain to meaning became steadily more acute. The self-harming side of the bargain was being fulfilled – Brexit would have plenty of suffering to deliver to those who voted for it. But the sadistic side was not – there was no clear target for the compensatory infliction of harm. Or perhaps one should say, not yet: the need to hurt someone else is the dangling, unfinished business of Brexit's sadopopulist project.

In the meantime, as an elite form of neurotic escapism,

there was one last refuge for self-pity: leave the plebs in their bondage trousers and return to the Middle Ages. A strange word re-entered English public discourse, its sudden presence a reminder that there was still some mileage in the ridiculous at the heart of Brexit's sublime. That word was vassalage: 'the state or condition of a vassal; subordination, homage or allegiance characteristic of or resembling that of a vassal'.[33]

6.

THE TWILIGHT OF THE GODS: ENGLISH DREAMTIME

Like the gods of myth in the same physical
environment as the ordinary, subject citizen,
but in a separate realm politically

—WILLIAM REES-MOGG

There is a thing that emerging nationalisms do. Since recent
history is always full of compromises, complexities and
contradictions, they seek out a version of the past that
is not history but myth. They imagine themselves back into
an aboriginal Dreamtime of gods and demigods. Wagner did
this for German nationalism in the nineteenth century. Irish
nationalism dreamed itself back into the mythological time
of Cúchulainn and Fionn MacCumhaill. William Blake even
tried to do this for the English revolution that never happened
in the late eighteenth and early nineteenth centuries with his
elaborate prophetic myths of Albion. And at its most elite

levels Brexit takes refuge in its own English Dreamtime. Partly, this is a medieval time of 'vassalage' and marauding knights, a time, in the words of *Britannia Unchained*'s fantasy of liberated ultra-capitalism, 'when nearly all society's strictures are relaxed'. But it has, even beyond that, its own world of gods and demigods. What we have to understand is that these gods are the super-rich.

The promise of Brexit is, to borrow from T. S. Eliot, that 'history is now and England'. This is a promise of time and place: 23 June 2016 is a radiant moment in time and through it England becomes again a radiant place. But these promises, like all of Brexit's, turn out to be false. The moment of the referendum does not have a clear meaning – it is almost immediately lost in contention and confusion. But neither does 'England'. It emerges as a divided thing, bitterly split, not just between Leavers and Remainers but between the England of the big multi-cultural cities on the one side and the England of the villages and towns on the other. And so Brexit must inevitably exit its own condition, into mythological time. And it must acknowledge the true gods: the gods of international capital.

At stake here is an idea of sovereignty. It is the great appeal of Brexit: we are re-establishing our sovereignty, taking it back from Brussels. But it is also the great contradiction: if restoring sovereignty to Westminster and the British courts is the point of the exercise, why does the rhetoric of Brexit so quickly resolve itself into hysterical attacks on the exercise of this very sovereignty by Parliament and the Supreme Court? To escape this contradiction, there is recourse to the dark, deep past where sovereignty is befuddled by feudal notions of honour and duty. And, lying even further behind this, there is the spectre that the Brexit ultras are transfixed by: the Sovereign Individual.

Although they are about pain and self-harm in a decadent English upper class, the Patrick Melrose novels are largely set in a grand French chateau, as if the English aristocracy had won the Hundred Years War of the fourteenth and fifteenth centuries and established itself where it thought it belonged: in France. The monstrous father, David, has an antique, throne-like chair and in one of the novels, *Never Mind*, Patrick sees him sitting in it, 'striking a pose he remembered from the *Illustrated History of England* he had been given at prep school. The picture portrayed Henry V's superb anger when he was sent a present of tennis balls by the insolent King of France.'[1]

These tennis balls are an early, de luxe version of the prawn cocktail flavour crisp: trivial objects blown up to gigantic proportions as evidence of continental disdain for England and thus transformed in a *casus belli*. As Jonathan Sumption puts it in his magisterial history of the Hundred Years War, 'The story of the tennis balls, supposedly sent to Henry V by the Dauphin [not the king] with the message that he would do better to amuse himself at home than to meddle in France, was not just a conceit of Shakespeare's. Variants of it circulated in Henry's lifetime. It is a fable, but like many fables it contained a symbolic truth.'[2] In the first act of *Henry V*, Shakespeare has England's warrior-king go in a few lines from tennis balls to mass slaughter. He warns the French ambassadors that the Dauphin's joke 'Hath turned his balls to gunstones', transforming tennis balls into cannonballs:

... for many a thousand widows
Shall this mock mock out of their dear husbands,
Mock mothers from their sons, mock castles down...
His jest will savour but of shallow wit
When thousands more weep than did laugh at it.[3]

The same might be said for Brexit, another upper-class jest that
will end with more tears than laughter, and another upper-
class adventure in inflicting pain to toughen up England. The
sudden reappearance of 'vassalage' as an allegedly relevant
concept in English public discourse in 2018 tells us that in
the English ruling-class imagination, the Hundred Years War
– which was all about vassalage – is still being fought. Small
wonder, perhaps, that England struggles to escape from the
memory of the Second World War: its ruling class has not
even managed to get over a conflict that raged from the 1330s
to the final expulsion of the English from France in the middle
of the fifteenth century.

Maybe it didn't help that the EU's chief negotiator, Michel
Barnier, was French. In the Patrick Melrose novels, there is an
episode – brought to life in an exquisitely hideous sequence
in the 2018 TV adaptation – that serves as an almost pornographic English fantasy of humiliating the French. At an
aristocratic dinner, the pompous but insecure French Ambassador Jacques Alantour spills some venison sauce on Princess
Margaret's dress. She makes him kneel in front of her and try
to rub it off: '"There's still a spot here," said Princess Margaret
bossily, pointing to a small stain on the upper edge of her lap.
The ambassador hesitated. "Go on, wipe it up!"' Nicholas Pratt

describes the episode later to Melrose: 'Entre nous, I don't think the French have been so heroically represented since the Vichy government. You should have seen the way Alantour slid to his knees.'[4] Yet Pratt might easily have said, not 'since Vichy', but 'since Agincourt'.

If this seems far-fetched, consider Jacob Rees-Mogg, leader of the Brexit ultras in the House of Commons, reacting in July 2018 to Theresa May's White Paper setting out, at last, what her government was seeking to achieve in the negotiations with Barnier. Rees-Mogg described the White Paper as representing 'the greatest vassalage since King John paid homage to Philip II at Le Goulet in 1200'.[5] (The Hundred Years War may in fact have been too modern for him.) In his resignation speech the following week, Boris Johnson picked up the word: 'We are volunteering for economic vassalage not just in goods and agri-foods but we will be forced to match EU arrangements on the environment and social affairs and much else besides.'[6]

The related term 'vassal state' had already become a staple of the Brexiteer lexicon. Given Russian interference in the Brexit vote, it is interesting that this use of 'vassal state' picked up on the rhetoric of Vladimir Putin. Speaking in 2014 at his annual press conference in Moscow, Russia's president accused the United States and Europe of deciding 'that they are winners, they are an empire now and the rest are vassals and they have to be driven into a corner'.[7] But in any case, the notion that England was returning to an essentially feudal conflict was common currency by early 2018. The *Express* columnist Leo McKinstry wrote, 'We are sliding towards the status of a regional province of a feudal superstate... Jacob Rees-Mogg says there is now a real danger Britain could become nothing more than a "vassal state" during the transition.'[8] The *Telegraph*'s headline in August 2017 over Martin Howe's piece on post-Brexit legal arrangements was 'We are not a vassal state, and we should not be ruled by Europe's vassal court': 'The EFTA Court is in effect a vassal court which transmits ECJ rulings downwards to the EEA countries. They have chosen effectively to make themselves vassal states of the EU, bound by its rules but with no vote on them.'[9]

This is the obverse of Rees-Mogg's rallying cry at the Tory Party conference in October 2017, framing Brexit as a continuation of the great triumphs of English arms on continental Europe: 'We need to be reiterating the benefits of Brexit!... Oh, this is so important in the history of our country... It's Waterloo! It's Crécy! It's Agincourt! We win all these things!'[10] Agincourt was undoubtedly a great feat of arms, and its 600th anniversary in October 2015 – marked among other things by a royal ceremony at Westminster Abbey at which Henry V's sword was held aloft in procession and an actor in medieval military gear delivered some of the pre-battle speech that Shakespeare put in his mouth – had given it renewed currency in the run-up to the Brexit vote. The anguished evocation of English 'vassalage' in 2018 was inextricable from the idea that the glory of Crécy and Agincourt deserved a better reward.

There is something both deeply neurotic and accidentally honest about this. Neurotic because it is an upper-class, gold-plated version of the way in which England's failure to get its just deserts from victory in the Second World War fed masochistic fantasies of defeat. Honest because in reality these glorious medieval victories were part of a war that was disastrous at every level. It was an elite project that mobilized popular patriotism while draining the people's resources. Its overall effects are summarized by Jonathan Sumption: 'In England, it brought intense effort and suffering, a powerful tide of patriotism, great fortune succeeded by bankruptcy, disintegration and utter defeat.'[11] A perfect preview of the long-term effects of Brexit, at least for the masses: if 'We always win these things', it depends very much on who the 'we' is.

But the beauty of medieval England is that it is so far off in time that you can make up whatever you want about it. Making stuff up about medieval England has a curious place in the genealogy of Brexit. Boris Johnson's spectacular career in public mendacity actually began with it. Key documents in his ascent are two 'news' reports in *The Times*, written in May 1988 when he was a graduate trainee on the paper: 'Edward II's "Rosary" Palace found in London', published on 20 May and 'Timber may show date of Edward II's palace' four days later. Johnson reported on an archaeological dig apparently discovering 'the long-lost palace of King Edward II' on the South Bank of the Thames: 'According to Dr Colin Lucas, of Balliol College, Oxford, this is where the king enjoyed a reign of dissolution with his catamite, Piers Gaveston, before he was gruesomely murdered at Berkeley Castle by barons who felt he was too prone to foreign influence.' The second article rebuked Lucas for these claims, with their delicious artificial flavourings of homophobia, xenophobia and 'fifth column' paranoia: 'Dr Colin Lucas of Balliol College Oxford said "Edward II is reputed to have led a life of wine and song with his catamite Piers Gaveston." But if 1325 is correct [as a date for the building of the Rosary Palace] this could hardly have taken place in this building since Gaveston was executed in 1312.'

Colin Lucas is a genuine Oxford historian (though of modern France), and is in fact Johnson's godfather. But Boris had simply made up these quotes and attributed them to him, with the added effrontery that when his own ignorance was revealed in the process he simply made up a second quote to cover it. When Lucas complained, Johnson was fired. But his career was launched. He was immediately hired by the *Daily Telegraph* as its correspondent in Brussels where his talent for lurid invention came into its own. The moral of the story for ambitious Tories was clear enough: making stuff up about fourteenth-century England is a good career move.

As it happens, though, there is a valid reason to return to vassalage, Crécy and Agincourt in the context of Brexit. For in England's very long history as a nation state – much longer than most current political entities can claim – there is just one episode that is more thoroughly unhinged than Brexit. The Hundred Years War is one of the great criminal follies of European history: repeated English invasions of France that unleashed on innocent civilians mass murder, mass rape, theft on a staggering scale and an orgy of destruction. It brought nothing but horror and misery. And all in the failed pursuit of a mad idea rooted in elite concerns with face and honour.

On 26 January 1340, the English king Edward III stood on a platform in the marketplace of Ghent in Flanders. It was bedecked with new banners commissioned from the workshops of Antwerp, showing the arms of England quartered with those of France. And from that platform Edward declared himself King of France. A Florentine merchant who was there asked some of the locals what they thought. The better sort, he reported, thought the whole thing 'puerile'.[12] But for almost half a millennium, until 1802, the English monarchs would go on claiming to be kings of France.

Edward was not mad. He knew the claim wasn't real. He made it because he was in dispute with the actual French monarchy about the feudal status of his own vast holdings in the south-west of the country, the duchy of Aquitaine. He was offended that he held these lands in – and here the term has its contemporary resonances – vassalage to the French king. But – and here the ludicrousness of those contemporary resonances is revealed – the vassal state was not England. It was Aquitaine. The whole horror show was never about English sovereignty. It was about an aristocratic elite's anxiety about its own status.

Edward needed the support of the Flemings, but they were also feudal subjects of the French monarchy. They couldn't support him unless he declared that he was in fact King of France. So he did. This raises, though, one of the great problems of Brexit: saving face. People – and states – don't act merely out of self-interest. There are times when they make claims they know to be daft, but they can't find a way to back down.

The claim that the English monarch was King of France started out as a tactic for dealing with an immediate political problem, just as Brexit has its origins in David Cameron's strategy for dealing with internal dissent in the Tory Party. It, too, was thought of as a kind of deliberate overreach: Edward, like the less extreme of the Brexiteers, thought he was making an exaggerated gesture that could be bargained away in later negotiations. But, like them, he miscalculated. As Sumption puts it, 'Edward always overrated the bargaining value of his claim to the French throne, and he was unwilling to abandon it until the French King's obligations had been performed to the last letter.'[13]

But neither Edward nor his successors could find the right means to step down from the platform that he constructed in Ghent in 1340. The consequences were appalling. The repeated invasions of France cost English lives and sucked up English resources. They disrupted and at times destroyed the trade with Flanders and France that had been so important to the English economy. The insatiable demand for taxation to pay for them very nearly destroyed the English state in the Peasants' Revolt of 1381. But for the ordinary people of France, the Low Countries, Spain and Italy (all of which were drawn into the conflict) the suffering was immense and seemingly interminable.

The fabulous English military victories at Crécy and Agincourt, at Sluys and Poitiers, did not end the war. As Jonathan Sumption puts it, they simply 'underlined the essential unimportance of battles as a means of achieving anything of long-term significance'.[14] The English state could not hold conquered territory for long or sustain a large standing army. Its solution was one that would appeal to most of the free-market ultras behind Brexit: the war was privatized and outsourced to gangsters, for whom, truly, 'nearly all society's strictures are relaxed'. Sumption (interestingly, now a member of the UK's Supreme Court) calls the English strategy 'terrorism on a great scale'.[15]

Warlords were unleashed on the general population. Edward himself described these men as 'outlaws, criminals, murderers, thieves'. The contemporary English knight Sir Thomas Gray called them 'a horde of yobs'.[16]

They stormed towns, raping and killing. They enslaved men and women. They held anyone they thought had money for ransom and tortured them until their families paid up. They stole everything that could be moved and destroyed most of what could not. When they had stripped an area of everything, they moved on to the next set of victims – all in the name of the English 'king of France'.

But even the official English armies were savage. The Italian poet Petrarch, travelling through the area south of Reims a few months after the passage of the English army through it, wrote: 'Everywhere was grief, destruction, desolation, uncultivated fields filled with weeds, ruined and abandoned houses...'[17] Shakespeare, in *Henry V*, dramatizes the hero as the greatest of the English warrior-kings, but slips in an accurate description of the fate of civilians at the hands of his country's armies. Henry warns the people of Harfleur what will happen if they do not surrender: 'look to see/ The blind and bloody soldier with foul hand/ Defile the locks of your shrill-shrieking daughters;/ Your fathers taken by the silver beards,/ And their most reverend heads dash'd to the walls,/ Your naked infants spitted upon pikes.'

A cool observer might have said, *pace* the Charge of the Light Brigade: *C'est la guerre mais ce n'est pas magnifique.* This was all as glorious as the exploits of Joseph Kony (leader of the Lord's Resistance Army) in Uganda or Charles Taylor in

Sierra Leone in our time. And for what? At the end of all the suffering, English power in France had all but disappeared, the possessions that Edward III had started out with permanently lost to his successors. It is true that the English kings were no longer bound by vassalage for their domains in Aquitaine – but only because they no longer had any.

Even the worst Brexit will be nothing like the catastrophe of the Hundred Years War. But there are perhaps two meaningful parallels. One is the power of the big gesture. The English claim to the throne of France and the grand rhetoric of Brexit's revival of the glorious Englishness of Agincourt are bold and thrilling as well as being bonkers – they stir the blood even while they numb the brain. The other is that these grand gestures are far easier to make than to unmake. It is astonishing how much pain people will suffer and inflict rather than admit they made a mistake. Brexit is not the Hundred Years War, but unless someone finds a way out of it, the consequences will be felt for a century.

These are not the lessons intended to be drawn from the evocation of Brexit as Agincourt and a bad Brexit as the vassalage from which it was meant to free England. But, ludicrous as it is, this metaphor does illuminate three key aspects of the whole project after the referendum: the problem of social class, the problem of the Union and the problem of Englishness. The 'we' who always win is a slippery entity.

The most obvious thing is that talk of vassalage is meaningless to the vast majority of the population of the UK. Linguistically, it reeks of Eton and Oxbridge. Conceptually, it refers to the legal relationships between members of a super-rich caste.

Historically, it refers to a long series of episodes in which a feudal overlord class stripped England of men and money in a disastrous pursuit of its own dynastic ambitions. To put it mildly, it does not have the deep resonances of the Second World War, with all its memories of moral worth and social solidarity. The retreat into this metaphor therefore hints at the fundamental tension in Brexit – the profound differences in the self-interest and ideology of its leadership on the one hand, and the actual interests of their working-class followers on the other.

Secondly, in evoking the Hundred Years War as a rallying point, the Brexiteers seem unaware of a rather salient fact: Scotland was on the other side. In Shakespeare's *Henry V*, the warrior-king, before he sets off to avenge the insult of the tennis balls, warns his court to be on guard against the Scots who will almost certainly attack across England's northern frontiers. Which indeed they did – Scotland was allied throughout most of the long war with France. Crécy and Agincourt were not Scots victories on the battlefield, they were Scots defeats. 'We' didn't win because in the context of Britain (as opposed to England) there was no we, only them and us.

That this would not occur to the leading Brexiteers is a mark of the great gulf between their passionate commitment to the Union on the one side and their ignorance of and indifference to Scotland on the other. It also marks a decline in the unifying power of the myth of heroic failure. At its height, it really did appeal, not just to the English but to pretty much all of the peoples of what was then the United Kingdom of Great Britain and Ireland. Scottish dissenters had their own embodiment of the myth in the missionary explorer David Livingstone. Even militant Irish nationalists could turn it to their own account as they did with the Easter Rising of 1916. But attempts to glorify the disaster of the Hundred Years War have no such power. To the extent that they resonate at all outside of upper-class culture, they do so only in England. As such they give the game away – Brexit is at heart an English nationalist project.

But even here the use of the metaphor points towards a fundamental uncertainty in English identity as it relates to continental Europe: is England an island or is it not? The point of the Hundred Years War was to prove that it is not, that it extends into Normandy and Aquitaine and (in principle) into the whole of France. But this has no emotional appeal: insularity is what defines post-imperial English identity. If one were to ask most Brexiteers for a piece of poetry that summed up their patriotic feelings, it would probably be John of Gaunt's mesmerizing evocation of a sacred England in *Richard II*:

> This royal throne of kings, this scepter'd isle,
> This earth of majesty, this seat of Mars,
> This other Eden, demi-paradise,
> This fortress built by Nature for herself
> Against infection and the hand of war,
> This happy breed of men, this little world,
> This precious stone set in the silver sea...

There could be no more stirring evocation of Fortress England as a perfect 'little world'. The imagined community of post-

Brexit England is John of Gaunt's demi-paradise, a place uniquely carved out by nature to protect its happy breed from the infection of foreigners. But even as you read these lines you stumble over the word 'isle'. Gaunt in this speech is talking explicitly about 'this realm, this England' – not about Britain. And England isn't an island. The speech keeps claiming the idea of a land surrounded by water, 'bound in with the triumphant sea'. Gaunt's geography is strangely out of kilter. And so is Shakespeare's history. When the actual people of England rose up in the Peasants' Revolt, John of Gaunt was at the top of their hit list. He was Jean of Ghent, as in the city that is now part of Belgium. He was a French-speaking Plantagenet who spent much of his time in Aquitaine and became, for fifteen years, titular King of Castile.

And this contradiction recurs in modern political constructions of Englishness. On the one hand, England is a non-island that celebrates its insularity. As James Morris wrote in 1962 in the debate on possible membership of the Common Market, 'Half the fun of being English is being an islander, but only the stuffiness of insularity is emphasised, never the exhilaration.'[18] When a decision was taken not to build the Channel Tunnel, the Labour minister Barbara Castle wrote in her diary for 16 January 1975: 'I am relieved that [Environment Secretary] Tony Crosland has decided we cannot go ahead. This is not only anti-Common Market prejudice. It is a kind of earthy feeling that an island is an island and should not be violated. Certainly I am convinced that the building of a tunnel would do something profound to the national attitude – and certainly not for the better. There is too much facile access being built into the modern world.'[19] Castle's sense of violation was echoed in the phrase used by Randolph Churchill when in opposition to the renewed (and successful) proposal for a tunnel in June 1988, he evoked the need for Britain to remain 'virgo intacta'.[20]

This may be the fantasy world of the popular Brexit, but it does not belong in the elite version, which still imagines an England that extrudes into France as it did in the glory days of the fourteenth century. After the Brexit referendum, Boris Johnson could use the pipedream of filling in the Channel as an argument that no formal ties to Europe were necessary because there was really no separation:

> For those who really want to make Britain less insular, the answer is not to submit forever to the EU legal order, but to think about how we can undo the physical separation that took place at the end of the Ice Age. Fly over the Channel at Dover and you see how narrow it is, the ferries plying back and forth like buses in Oxford Street, and as you measure the blue straits with your fingers you can see that this moat is really an overgrown prehistoric river that once flowed down from Norway and was fed by its tributaries, the Thames and the Seine and the Rhine.[21]

When the Channel is paved over, the scepter'd isle will physically reconnect with its Angevin dynastic destiny.

But this bizarre medievalist whimsy has an even stranger counterpart, a notion that pushes it further beyond the living complications of time and space and into mythic Dreamtime. This is where we encounter the world of the gods.

When England was anxiously debating where it belonged in the context of Europe, Arthur Koestler sardonically suggested that 'all they will have to do is to enlist a battalion of frogmen. The frogmen will cut the moorings of these islands, and tow them to Botany Bay, or the shores of New Zealand.'[22] This has not yet been put forward as a solution by the Brexiteers but it has a strange relevance – both literally and metaphorically.

At the heart of Brexit's appeal to most of those who voted for it was an idea of national sovereignty and a sense of place. But, in fact, one of the underlying motives for the elite that created it is a desire to shake both of these off. For most of those who voted for it, Brexit means a 'return to the nation state'. But for many of those behind it, there is a very different ideal. They use this language because it is the only one that is politically viable. But for them the exit from the EU is really a prelude to the exit from the nation state into a world where the rich are truly free because they are truly stateless.

A key Brexit text is a book published in 1997 by Jacob Rees-Mogg's father William (written with James Dale Davidson). Its title is telling: *The Sovereign Individual*. It is an avowedly apocalyptic mess of Ayn Rand-ish prognostications, addressed quite explicitly to the super-rich. And what it argues is that the millennial year 2000 would mark the dawn of a new age, one in which sovereignty would pass to these super-rich individuals and nation states would die.

While the rhetoric of Brexit attacked 'citizens of nowhere', Rees-Mogg senior argued that this is precisely what the ultra-wealthy titans of the new age can and must be. The book is, as it says, a manifesto for the '"cognitive elite" who operate outside the boundaries of nation states and political systems and feel equally at home in Frankfurt, Hong Kong, Tokyo or New York.[23] This elite will, in the early twenty-first century, free itself from all the constraints of nationality, citizenship and, of course, taxation. Thus the nation state itself will not survive.[24] It will 'starve to death as its tax revenues decline' because the new elite have declared themselves sovereign and are thus no longer taxable. Mass democracy and the concept of citizenship will be left behind: 'It is... only a matter of time until mass democracy goes the way of its fraternal twin, Communism.'[25]

This connects to the cod-medievalism of Rees-Mogg senior's son Jacob. The model for the new elite proposed by William Rees-Mogg is that of the military orders of medieval Europe like the Knights Templar and the Order of Malta who operated without regard to nationality, made their own laws and could 'control considerable wealth and military power without controlling any fixed territory' and 'in no sense derived their authority from national identity'.[26]

But they will not just be men – they will be gods. The 'good news for the rich' is that 'What mythology described as the province of the gods will become a viable option for the individual – a life outside the reach of kings and councils. First in scores, then in hundreds, and ultimately in the millions, individuals will escape the shackles of politics. As they do, they will transform the character of governments, shrinking the realm of compulsion and widening the scope of private control over resources.'[27]

These divine Sovereign Individuals will 'operate like the gods of myth in the same physical environment as the ordinary, subject citizen, but in a separate realm politically'.[28] The book talks of 'the tyranny of place' and of 'transcending locality'.[29] It spells out what this will mean: the seceding elites will establish their own enclaves, microstates independent of any existing country. And, of course, 'The lower classes will be walled out. The move to gated communities is all but inevitable. Walling out troublemakers is an effective as well as traditional way of minimising criminal violence in times of weak central authority.'[30]

Within these walled microstates, 'control over economic resources will shift away from the state to persons of superior skills and intelligence'. Beyond them, in the now withered nation states where welfare systems and public services have collapsed because tax revenue has dried up, will dwell the majority of 'losers and left-behinds' too dumb to rise to Sovereign Individual status: 'New survival strategies for persons of lower intelligence will evolve, involving greater concentration on development of leisure skills, sports abilities, and crime, as well as service to the growing numbers of Sovereign Individuals.'[31] These mere humans will serve the gods, one assumes, as cleaners, prostitutes and gladiators.

Crazed as this might be, it was intended as a practical programme. *The Sovereign Individual* has an appendix offering services – an investment vehicle in Bermuda, membership of an offshore trust, advice on how to 'secure your own tax-free zone' and membership of The Sovereign Society, composed of 'would-be Sovereign Individuals… who have clubbed together to help one another achieve independence'.[32] (The desire for self-governing enclaves for the ultra-rich is an active project for the Trump-supporting tech billionaire Peter Thiel, who wants to create a marine republic for the elite off the coast of California.)

Crucial in this dystopian/utopian vision is the idea of exit. Rees-Mogg senior wrote that even in the early stages of this new age many wealthy citizens of Western democracies were already, like people in East Berlin in 1989, planning their exodus: 'abandoning the country of their birth is not [an] unthinkable decision'.[33] The nation state, for these new gods, is a 'predatory institution' from which 'the individual will want to escape'.[34] Rees-Mogg identified New Zealand as an ideal location for this new post-national elite, a 'domicile of choice for wealth creation in the Information Age'. In the mid-1990s, a giant sheep station at the southern tip of the North Island was purchased by a conglomerate whose major shareholders included Davidson and Rees-Mogg.[35] Koestler's joke about towing England off to New Zealand thus had a kind of loopy reality in a fever-dream of elite escape from the shackles of the nation and responsibilities to anyone except oneself.

Jacob Rees-Mogg is not his father, but he is his father's son in three respects. One is that, behind his English nationalism, he too fervently believes in the sovereignty of the super-rich and their right to escape. In June 2018, Somerset Capital Management, which he co-owns, launched a Dublin-based tax-efficient 'collected asset vehicle' investment structure to ensure that it could continue to operate under the EU regulations he decries as oppressive. The following month, he launched a second Dublin-based fund 'to meet demand from international investors' concerned about the effects of Brexit.[36]

For all the talk of national sovereignty, in his real world it is the super-rich individual who exerts a transnational sovereignty. For the gods, there is always an exit – even from Brexit. Secondly, like most of the Brexit ultras, his hatred of the EU is primarily rooted in its restraint of buccaneering capitalism. Thirdly, like his father, with his notion of Sovereign Individuals banding together in their own transnational orders like medieval knights, he can't resist a feudal metaphor.

What, then, is the appeal of vassalage? George Orwell put it best: 'Given the *fact* of servitude, the feudal relationship is the only tolerable one.'[37] In Brexit, just as the long dreams of invasion ultimately produced actual planning for a revisiting of wartime, so the fantasy of vassalage opens up a possible reality. The very people who indulged in it led Britain towards the tangible possibility that it would indeed become a kind of satellite of the EU, having to accept its rules and regulations without having a say in making them. This would be a very mild form of subservience, but being subject to laws one does not have a part in making is indeed a good definition of what political subordination looks like. 'The *fact* of servitude' was one created entirely by the Brexiteers themselves.

But having created the real possibility of a form of servitude, it was more tolerable if it were dressed up as a feudal relationship. More tolerable in part because this would remove it from the very recent history that had actually led to it – the living history of opportunism, recklessness, fantasy and cynicism – and hive it off into a historical Dreamtime, a faraway past of which we (or at least Johnson and Rees-Mogg) know next to nothing. It is highly improbable that the vast majority of the people of England in 1200 knew or cared that King John paid homage to Philip II at Le Goulet – and entirely certain that the vast majority of the people of England neither knew nor cared in 2018. But as an alternative way of explaining how their state had ended up in the wilderness mapped by Theresa May's White Paper, it was better than the truth.

And Rees-Mogg's reference to Le Goulet did have that killer word 'homage'. This was the other thing that made the idea of a feudal relationship more tolerable than the facts of a messy, ambiguous, mutually unsatisfactory affiliation between the UK and the EU after Brexit. It made the whole thing a matter of honour. England was not involved in tedious, complex and inevitably disappointing negotiations in order to find the least worst compromise and make the best of a very bad job. It was being insulted. It demanded cake and Barnier sent it tennis balls. The duty of the people of England when the honour of its rulers was at stake was always plain: to suffer gloriously for as long as it took for the whole thing to peter out in exhaustion and futility. Rees-Mogg suggested that the rewards of Brexit might be fully apparent in fifty years' time, but, given his expansive sense of history, why not make it a hundred? Or, as happens in Dreamtime, in the long never-never.

7.

THE SORE TOOTH AND THE BROKEN UMBRELLA

… Nothing we know explains
the vague geography tingling in our veins

—DEREK MAHON

The quintessential English film is the 1969 comedy *The Italian Job*, a movie for which the word 'caper' might have been invented. Ask most English people for their favourite line from a movie, and they'll do Michael Caine's Cockney bark when his dumb sidekick Arthur has just accidentally blown a security van to smithereens by remote control: 'You're only supposed to blow the bloody doors off!' It was the line that Michael Gove's wife, Sarah Vine, thought of when she woke him on the morning after the Brexit referendum to inform him that Leave had actually won: 'Michael reappeared, towelling the water from his hair. By now his phone was buzzing and beeping like a demented frog. "You were only supposed to blow

173

the bloody doors off," I said, in my best (i.e. not very good) Michael Caine *Italian Job* accent. In other words, you've really torn it now.'[1]

It helped, perhaps, that Caine himself is an enthusiastic Brexiteer, a multimillionaire who declares that poverty is more noble for other Britons than subjection to the EU's 'faceless dictators': 'I voted for Brexit. I'd rather be a poor master than a rich servant.'[2] As Gove told the *Sun*: 'I love Michael Caine. He's the kind of expert I like.' The odd thing is that the line is more truthful than so much of the subsequent official rhetoric about Brexit. In the film, it is about screwing up. Caine delivers it to Michael Standing's cloth-capped Arthur, the epitome of English overconfidence. We have just seen Arthur blithely press the button to trigger the explosion with a gormless grin on his face. And we watch his expression turn to stupid embarrassment as the van is blasted into oblivion. It is Arthur, not Michael Caine, who is really the kind of expert the Brexiteers like.

But for many of those who voted Leave, the intention surely was only to blow the doors off. The referendum was an opportunity to vent a general rage at the Establishment, much of it justified. It was a free flying kick at the well-upholstered bums. But instead of being a controlled explosion of anger, it sent the whole vehicle of state skywards. Brexit just has too much gelignite packed into it – its destructive energy is not properly contained because it is, in part, misplaced.

There is, moreover, an equally famous line from *The Italian Job* and it suggests a very different metaphor. If the explosion scene seemed to sum up the giddy mood in 2016, the end of the movie is perfect for Britain's precarious position two years later as it tried to reassemble a viable vehicle from the wreckage. After the successful heist, the getaway driver (interestingly, the only black character in the film) loses control on winding mountain roads of the bus into which the gold bullion has been loaded. The back of the bus is left teetering over a cliff and the gold slides towards the rear doors. The final moments of the movie are post-referendum Brexit in a two-minute cameo. We see the stacks of gold bars stolen in the audacious heist, with a Union Jack planted on top of them – the fabulous future of the post-Brexit trading empire. But as Michael Caine's Croker attempts to reach the gold, its full weight slips further towards the back, threatening to tip the bus off the cliff and into the abyss below. The members of the crew (the Brexit mob) have to stay at the far side of the bus to act as a counterweight – otherwise the whole thing plunges off. They dare not move either forwards or backwards.

Caine turns around to them and delivers the final line: 'Hang on a minute, lads, I've got a great idea.' But these often-quoted words are not in fact his last utterances. As the music swells we hear his great idea: 'Uh, uh...' There is no great idea. In 2009, the Royal Society of Chemistry in the UK ran a competition asking members of the public to suggest solutions to the *Italian Job* dilemma. The winner came up with a very complex suggestion that involved, among other things, deflating the tyres and draining the fuel tanks. But as other members of the public were quick to point out, if the tyres are deflated and there is no fuel in the tanks, you can't drive the bus away with the gold in it. In truth, the gang either has to abandon its dreams of riches or plunge to its death.

The fascination of the film is that it was always metaphorical. To watch it now is to be struck by how self-consciously it deals with the tensions of English identity on the eve of Britain's entry to the Common Market. Deals with but does not resolve – it imagines the country's European future as a literal cliffhanger. That last scene is not accidental. This European caper teeters between cocky optimism and profound anxiety. This is an idea of something that might go either way, of opposite possibilities that cannot yet be synthesized into any coherent narrative.

On the one hand, the film is all about going into Europe. The last thing we see onscreen is not the bus teetering over the cliff, it is an acknowledgement of trans-European co-operation: 'Our Grateful thanks to the city of Turin and to Fiat for their help with this film'. *The Italian Job* is even prescient about economic globalization: the gold bars that are the object of the heist are a Chinese investment in Fiat. The centre of the movie is, moreover, an interaction, not of humans, but of industrial machines. It is a cinematic ballet in which the dancers are automobiles: the unabashedly red, white and blue Mini Coopers of the English robbers versus the Fiats of the Italian police. And there is no question about where superiority lies: the Minis – cool, sleek and lithe – trip a light fandango through the alleys and malls, across rooftops and even a river, while the Fiats stumble and crash in their wake. In an era when car manufacturing was the benchmark of national industrial might, *The Italian Job* is swaggeringly optimistic about Britain's coming dominance over the Europeans. Its dazzling cars will lead a new, peaceful invasion of

European markets. All the unfinished business of the war –
the Italians were, of course, enemies at the outset – will now
be resolved in a new victory for British engineering, design
and ingenuity.

On the other hand, though, the movie is deeply fearful.
It is rather startling to recall that a key moment in the plot
concerns precisely the anxiety that was leading most of the
British Establishment towards a reluctant decision to reapply
for membership of the Common Market: the balance of payments deficit. Noël Coward plays Bridger, whom we understand to be the emperor of the English criminal world. He
is in prison but completely in control of the governor, the
warders and the other lags. He is, in effect, the government –
imperious, commanding and ultrapatriotic. It is Bridger who
must sanction the Turin raid, much as Elizabeth I would have
licensed Francis Drake and other buccaneers. At first, he refuses
to do so. But then he demands that his sidekick bring him
the official balance of payments reports. We actually see him
reading through the statistics. He decides that Britain's situation is so desperate that it needs this gold from Turin. The
bullion is not a mere private reward for the criminals – it is an
act of sanctioned governmental piracy.

The European adventure thus hovers between swaggering
self-confidence and last-resort desperation. This is why the
film can have no clear ending: its mood is fundamentally
indeterminate. Is it a celebration of 'going into Europe'?
Or a Swinging London version of Agincourt, a hit-and-run
raid on the damn continentals in which the point is not just
to administer a good thrashing to the foreigners but to get

back safely to Blighty? But within this profound uncertainty, there is one very clear movement – Britishness becomes Englishness.

When Shakespeare imagined his version of Agincourt in *Henry V*, he went to considerable pains to make the gang British, not English: the Irishman Macmorris, the Scot Jamey and the Welshman Llewelyn have prominent parts. Since *The Italian Job* is a kind of revisiting of *Henry V*, it might seem obvious that Michael Caine's gang would have at least a token Jock, Taffy and/or Paddy, especially as the film was written by a Scot. But it doesn't. And as the film progresses, images of Britishness – the Union flag, the Queen – are gradually displaced by the red and white of England. The gang pose as England football fans (an international match is conveniently taking place in Turin) and wear the England colours. 'England for Me' is written on the side of their van. When word gets through to the prison that the job has been pulled off, we see Bridger processing majestically down the stairs while the entire population of cons and warders hails him with ecstatic chants of 'England! England!' In the midst of the unresolvable anxieties about Britain's future in Europe, it was Englishness, not Britishness, that offered comfort and certainty.

In 1962, when Britain was making its first attempt to join the Common Market, the Scottish-born writer and newspaper editor John Douglas Pringle noted astutely that England would be going through the same process that Scotland had endured when it entered a larger union in the eighteenth century. It seemed to him then that Scotland had essentially lost its identity in the United Kingdom:

Scotland had disappeared. It was 'the end of an auld sang'. ...
Some of us still cling to a Scottish culture which has lost its
virtue. Some of us have adopted an English culture which
we do not truly share or understand. The rest have created
a composite 'British' culture which even now is phony and
fictitious.

This, Pringle suggested, was what the English would have to
face in an evolving European union:

So to-day, when we watch the English making the same
decision ... Sympathy is mixed with a slight but unmistakable
Schadenfreude. We are like an old man, long impotent, who
sees a famous lecher buying erotic pictures in the Charing
Cross Road. How are the mighty fallen![3]

Pringle presciently suggested that since the Scots had already
lost their national identity, entry into Europe would not bother
them and that, if anything, it might even help Scotland to recover
its 'sense of distinction'. But he wondered whether the English
had really thought about what would happen to their sense of
national identity and how it related to questions of sovereignty.

Pringle had no more answers to these questions than
anyone else, but he was prescient in three important respects.
He was right that Scotland, which seemed to have dissolved
itself into Great Britain, could recover its 'sense of distinction'
in a European union. Right that Britishness itself might
come to seem for many English people, as it already seemed
for many Scots, 'phony and fictitious'. And right, too, that

England might end up buying erotic pictures of itself. He did not anticipate that they would have a sadomasochistic bent, but it was true that, in joining Europe, English identity would eventually become more like that of previously subject peoples. Colonized peoples end up making pictures of themselves in stimulating poses, performing a version of themselves that is overly self-conscious, hyperreal, exaggerated in its sense of difference. So would the English.

There is nothing at all strange or innately disreputable about English nationalism. England is arguably the oldest nation state – by the fourteenth century it had a common vernacular, a territory whose existence was not purely the result of dynastic ownership, a functioning central state and an aggressive sense of itself that could mobilize popular opinion. What is unusual is the process whereby this very powerful collective sense of belonging was folded into two other, closely related identities: Britishness and Empire. There was nothing natural or easy about this. It was slow, difficult and very deliberate.

We can see it at work in, for example, the work of William Shakespeare. After the accession of James VI of Scotland as James I of England, Shakespeare became a royal servant and his company became the King's Men. One of his jobs was to serve James's need for the invention of Britishness. As James Shapiro writes, 'Shakespeare had spent much of his career writing about Englishness; indeed a strong claim can be made that his nine Elizabethan English history plays did much to define English identity, if not English exceptionalism. That changed after he became a King's Man and his attention, and that of his Jacobean audiences, turned from Englishness to Britishness.' The word

'England' had appeared 224 times in Shakespeare's Elizabethan plays, but in the decade after James I took the throne, it appeared only twenty-nine times – mostly in the unavoidable historical context of his late collaborative history play *Henry VIII*. Likewise, 'English' appeared 132 times in the Elizabethan plays, but just eighteen times in the Jacobean works. Conversely, Shakespeare never once used the word 'British' before James's accession and 'Britain' occurred only twice. But in *King Lear* alone, 'Britain' is referred to three times and in the Jacobean plays 'British' is used twenty-nine times. As Shapiro puts it, 'In turning from Englishness to Britishness, Shakespeare was responding to questions that hadn't much interested his fellow countrymen before the arrival of King James.'[4]

This sublimation of Englishness into Britishness was, eventually, a great success. It worked because England was such a dominant partner in the Union that 'England' could be used – to the impotent irritation of the Scots and Welsh – as a synonym for Britain. And because the construction of the United Kingdom bought the peace and stability on the home island that allowed for the construction of a global empire. But this was a contract and neither of these key terms and conditions could be fulfilled for ever. By the beginning of the present century, the rise of Scottish, and to a lesser extent Welsh, nationalism radically altered the terms of the Union. And the Empire was gone. In retrospect, it was inevitable that the idea of England as a distinct political community would re-emerge. Like Reginald Perrin in one of the most popular English sitcoms of the years after entry to the Common Market, English nationalism would turn out to have faked its own death.

This should have been clear at least from the turn of the century. Historians of modern Britain understood it very well. Richard Weight, for example, wrote of the English in 2002: 'Dazed and confused by the changes which have taken place, they are not sure what they want... They have woken up en masse to the fact that their blithe unionism is no longer reciprocated and that their seamless Anglo-British identity is effectively redundant. Devolution has forced the English to do what their partners did in the second half of the twentieth century – to reconsider who they are as a people.'[5] But for the most part, the English political and media classes did little to help with this dazed confusion. While Irish, Scottish and Welsh nationalisms had long histories of political, artistic and cultural expression, English nationalism was largely left to its own devices.

Englishness had been both loud and silent, 'its roar', in the poet Thom Gunn's phrase, 'unheard from always being heard'. It was passionate, sometimes aggressive, always obvious, especially within the permissive arena of sport. Yet it was also largely unarticulated in and of itself, given political expression only in the fading disguise of an increasingly tattered British-ness. Early in the Second World War, George Orwell claimed in his survey of Englishness, *The Lion and the Unicorn*, that 'England is perhaps the only great country where intellectuals are ashamed of their own nationality'. It might be truer to say in the early twenty-first century that English intellectuals were ashamed, not of their nationality, but of their nationalism. English nationalism, not without reason, was seen as the prop-erty of skinheads, racists, football hooligans and drunken squaddies. A history of violence, domination and xenophobia made it radioactive. But it did not make it go away. The most dramatic evolution of national identity in Britain in the last two decades is the resurfacing of the idea of England as a distinct political community. But it is a great drama played out in small local venues, a national resurgence with no national arena to be performed in: until David Cameron blithely gave it a vast stage in June 2016.

Class prejudice may have been a factor in this: what George Orwell wrote in the 1940s – 'Hostile or friendly, nearly all the generalisations that are made about England base themselves on the property-owning class and ignore the other forty-five million'[6] – was scarcely less true sixty years later. A few artists and intellectuals – most notably Billy Bragg and Anthony Barnett – argued powerfully for the re-emerging Englishness to be taken seriously and given a positive democratic expression. A minority of political scientists risked accusations of eccentricity or worse to study it. What they found was startling – in retrospect perhaps so startling that it could be assumed to be untrue.

The key documents are *The Dog that Finally Barked*, published by the left-of-centre think-tank the Institute of Public Policy Research (IPPR) in 2012 and the follow-up report *England and Its Two Unions* in 2013. They pointed directly to 'the emergence of what might be called an "English political community", one marked by notable concerns within England about the seeming privileges of Scotland, in particular, in a devolved UK, a growing questioning of the capacity of the current UK-level political institutions to pursue and defend

English interests, and one underpinned by a deepening sense of English identity'.

In effect two very big and closely related things were going on – English people were choosing to be English rather than British and therefore becoming alienated from British governance. Firstly, the survey conducted in 2011 found that the proportion of the English population that prioritized an English over a British identity (40 per cent) was now more than twice as large as that which prioritized a British over an English identity (16 per cent).

This was not a rogue poll. The UK census taken in the same year was, if anything, even more emphatic. In England, fully 60 per cent of the population identified themselves as solely English. Remarkably, given that people could choose 'English' *and* 'British' if they wanted to, only 29 per cent of census participants in England identified themselves as feeling any sense of British national identity at all. In some parts of England, the embrace of an exclusively English identity is overwhelming: 70 per cent in the North East, 66 per cent in the North West, Yorkshire and the East Midlands.[7] By contrast, only 37 per cent of Londoners chose 'English only' – the cleavage between the metropolis and what Barnett calls 'England-without-London' that would be so obvious in the Brexit vote was already clear.

In European terms, this renewed English identity was highly significant. The 'English only' self-identification was much stronger than, for example, that of Bretons with Brittany or Galicians with Galicia. But the sheer speed of this shift is breathtaking and, perhaps, too rapid for politics and media to absorb. There were many factors at work, but the proximate cause was undoubtedly the establishment of the Scottish Parliament in 1999. In part, the new English nationalism is thus another example of the dominant power mimicking the gestures of small-nation 'liberation' movements – the English were reacting to and mirroring the emergence of a potent and effective Scottish nationalism.

Thus, in 1996, before the establishment of the Scottish Parliament, just a third of English people chose 'English' when they were asked to choose either 'British' or English' as the best description of their own identity. By 2011, asked the same question, half of them chose 'English'.[8] Conversely, a mere 16 per cent of English respondents in 2011 described themselves as either 'more British than English' or 'British not English' (many of them people of Caribbean or Asian ethnicity for whom Britishness was always a potentially more capacious identity). As the authors of the IPPR study put it, four years before the Brexit referendum, the evidence already pointed to 'the emergence in recent decades of a different kind of Anglo-British identity in which the "Anglo" component is increasingly considered the primary source of attachment for the English'.[9]

This seismic shift in national identity was also a revolution in identification with political institutions. There was a headlong plunge in English support for the basic proposition that 'England should be governed as it is now with laws made by the UK parliament'. In 1999, when the Scottish Parliament was just established, 62 per cent of English respondents agreed with this status quo. By 2008, this had fallen to a bare majority, 51 per cent. But by 2011, support for the status quo had collapsed even more dramatically to a mere 24 per cent and by 2012 it was down to 21 per cent. On the most fundamental question of democratic governance – who should make our laws? – over three-quarters of the English were out of sympathy with the existing arrangements. Instead, 36 per cent wanted England to be governed exclusively by English MPs at Westminster; 20 per cent wanted to be governed by a new English Parliament and 8 per cent wanted to see the establishment of devolved regional English Parliaments.[10]

This is a form of silent secession. In 1919, after Sinn Féin won the majority of Irish seats in the 1918 elections, it withdrew from Westminster and formed its own parliament in Dublin. This was easily understood as a defiant act of withdrawal from both the Empire and the Union. England in the early twenty-first century was seceding in its turn from Westminster and Whitehall. But there was no Sinn Féin, no Easter Rising to dramatize a moment of national resurrection, no W. B. Yeats to give it gravity and beauty.

The English revolution was conscious of itself: it is important to note that people in England knew that this was happening, even if most of the political and media establishments ignored it. In 2011, 60 per cent agreed to the proposition 'People in England have become more aware of English national identity'.[11] This self-awareness was also largely self-generated – tabloid jingoism, except when it came to sports that England played as a distinct country, remained 'British'. Even the most obvious vehicle for English nationalism hid itself behind the rubric of the UK Independence Party. As the IPPR authors put it, 'the strengthening and politicisation of English identity is taking place in the absence of any formal political mobilisation. Englishness, in other words, has a momentum of its own.'[12]

They were surely right to warn that 'the main problem is not that the English question is now finally being asked by the country's electorate, but rather the failure of the British political class to take it, and them, seriously'.[13] In 2014, Michael Kenny suggested that the re-emergence of English national identity 'may well turn out to constitute one of the most important phases in the history of the national consciousness of the English since the 18th century'.[14] But you wouldn't have known it from mainstream political and media discourse.

In one important respect, the English were now genuinely experiencing an irritation that had previously belonged only to the Scots, Irish and Welsh: the torment of naming. The English had long assumed the unconscious privilege of using 'English' as a synonym for 'British', driving the Scots in particular to distraction. (In 2016, for example, when the *Daily Mail* ran that screaming front-page headline 'Who will speak for England?' it explained in the small print of the editorial that 'of course... by "England" we mean the whole of the United Kingdom'.[15]) But as Britishness receded, the English themselves were left stranded in a kind of political anonymity. While they increasingly thought of themselves as English, Westminster and Whitehall were, as the authors of the IPPR report put it in 2013, 'seemingly unable to address the bulk of its citizenry by their chosen, collective name: "England"'.[16] Here, as Michael Gove in his Oscar Wilde pose might have noted, was a love that, officially at least, dared not speak its name.

What was happening from the turn of the century onwards,

therefore, was a secession with no clear idea of what was to be seceded *from*. Just one in five English people now consented to their current form of governance, but, as Anthony Barnett has articulated so well, they had no way to opt out of it: 'Unable to exit Britain, the English did the next-best thing and told the EU to fuck off.'[17] They had but one recourse: the act of secession itself. The long history of displacing onto the European Union the unresolved anxieties of England made possible a deft transference: if you can't secede from Britain, secede from Europe.

The transference was possible because people who identified primarily as English had a grossly exaggerated, camped-up sense of the extent to which they were being governed from Brussels. This rising English nationalism was different in many ways from the Scottish and Welsh varieties but one of the most obvious differentiations was perception of EU influence. When Scots and Welsh were asked to identity which layer of government had most influence over their lives, just 8 per cent and 7 per cent respectively cited the EU. This was very much typical of responses in regions throughout Europe from Bavaria to Brittany. The great exception was England, where 31 per cent of people cited the EU as the most influential layer of government (and just 1 per cent thought that it should have such influence).[18] Unsurprisingly, therefore, survey data showed a very strong link between identification as 'English only' and hostility to the EU. Fully 64 per cent of people with an exclusively English identity in 2012 said the EU was a 'bad thing', compared to just 28 per cent of those who chose a British-only identity.[19]

Equally unsurprising is that this translated into votes in June 2016. The IPPR authors had warned, 'It is English, rather than British, hackles that rise in response to Europe'[20] and they were proved entirely right. In England, outside of Greater London, the percentage of constituencies with Leave majorities varied from a low of 69 per cent in the South East and East Anglia to a high of fully 87.6 per cent in the Midlands.[21] And there is a very strong correlation between a sense of English identity and voting Leave: as Jan Eichhorn summarizes the evidence from the British Electoral Survey, 'People in England who feel strongly attached to their English national identity are much more likely to support Brexit than those who do not. Of those who chose the highest value for English identity on a 7-point scale, over 70 per cent voted to leave the EU. Conversely, over 80 per cent amongst those who only emphasise their English-ness slightly (2 on a 7-point scale) voted to remain.'[22]

Yet Brexit cannot be what it wants to be: England's Sinn Féin (the name means, roughly, 'Ourselves Alone') moment. It is an act of displacement. Anarchic rebellions are often like this – the peasants can't storm the castle and kill the lords, so they take it out on the petty clerks and the Jews and the foreign shopkeepers. Deeply disaffected with Westminster and White-hall, England-without-London unleashed its fury on Brussels and Strasbourg. Unable to name the 'us' of England, it was offered the chance to name the 'them' of the EU (and implicitly the real and imagined migrants that somehow embodied it) and took it. The problem is that the whole gesture is based on something imaginary: an enormous overstatement of the power of the EU in the governance of England.

And the overthrow of an imaginary oppressor cannot amount to an act of national liberation. Something big has been erased but nothing has really been revealed. Englishness is no better expressed after the Brexit vote than it was before it. If anything, the official rhetoric of 'defending the Union' has been ramped up to an ever-louder volume in the ensuing political panic. One of the great ironies of post-2016 politics is that Theresa May's disastrous election ended up giving a far louder and more insistent voice to a marginal expression of vestigial Britishness – that of Northern Ireland's DUP – than to the English nationalism that had been a primary factor in causing the earthquake.

For England, Brexit is a strange kind of resurrection: the tomb is empty but the vanished body has not been seen alive. English political identity has returned from the dead but it has not been allowed to show itself to its disciples. Or to use a less exalted metaphor, it is all rather like one of those animal movies, in which Lassie or Skippy comes bounding up making semi-articulate sounds of urgency and pointing frantically towards a scene of distress and the kids say, 'I think he's trying to tell us something!' Except that in this movie everybody then runs off in precisely the wrong direction.

One of the main responses of the Conservative government to the deep lacuna in political authority created by the Brexit vote was to reach for precisely what the people who voted for Brexit had been rejecting: an insistently unitary Britishness. To take a simple and symbolic example, the Brexiteers and their cheerleaders in the press would make much of the idea of restoring the blue-covered 'British passport' as an icon of independent identity. But asked in 2011 what nationality they would have on their passport if they could choose, fully 40 per cent of English respondents chose English.[23] There is good reason to think that these are the people who voted most enthusiastically for Brexit. Here we see one of the paradoxes and contradictions of Brexit itself. It is driven by a force – English nationalism – that its leaders still refuse to articulate. It draws on English disengagement from the Union, but wraps itself in a brashly reasserted Unionism.

This leaves England with the sore tooth problem. An unsettled and anxious sense of nationality is like having a sore tooth. The tooth is a very small part of the body and a sense of national identity is actually a very small part of most people's day-to-day lives. But a person with a toothache finds it hard to think about anything else. There is a pain that will not stop until it is somehow assuaged. Brexit is a huge operation (arguably performed under a general anaesthetic of mendacity) that deeply disturbs the entire body politic. But it is radically invasive surgery – not dentistry. It fulfils the old Yiddish curse: may all your teeth fall out except the one that gives you pain. It leaves the sore tooth just where it was. All it does is distract from the pain, much in the way that hitting your foot with a hammer will make you forget the ache in your tooth. Precisely because Brexit is fundamentally an act of displacement, nothing is surer than that the pain will return.

Indeed, pain is already built into Brexit, and not just in the obvious form of economic self-harm. It was always *intended* to fail. When, as already mentioned, in his call to tell David Cameron that he was going to campaign for Leave, Boris

Johnson assured the then prime minister that 'he doesn't expect to win, believing Brexit will be "crushed"', he was for once telling the truth. For a critical section of its supporters, and in particular for the effective leader of the Leave campaign, Brexit was always meant to be a Lost Cause. It would have been a jolly fine show, a splendid performance against insuperable odds. It would have the romance of, say, another great secession, the Confederacy in the southern states of the US: a thoroughly bad cause given a veneer of nobility by honourable defeat.

Except that, in its own postmodern way, Brexit is the Confederacy without the Civil War, a journey from cause to loss with nothing in between. Because it was based on fictions, because it had no plan, no internal agreement on what it wanted, no possibility of creating its own regime at Westminster and no possibility of negotiating with the EU an outcome that was better than the status quo, the question was not whether it would succeed but how badly it would fail. And then where else is there for it to go but into the Dreamland of what might have been? It will always be like the Confederacy for the white Deep South, in Frank Vandiver's words, an 'ideal which came, was fleetingly touched by life... and faded to the pantheon of lost glories' where 'the brief blood bath lent a strange endurance and gave hope to generations held tight in inertia, fear, poverty, and the horror of a lost dream and a shattered mirror'.[24]

This is one kind of highly possible English future. And it is made all the more possible because Lost Causism consoles itself with something that is also deeply rooted in the English tradition of Heroic Failure: the masochistic idea that the supreme expression of 'character' is the endurance of pain.

In the absence of a genuine political expression, 'character' itself is the great fall-back for a notion of Englishness. Most nations have stereotyped images of themselves but in England they seem to play an outsized role, precisely because they fill a gap where politics should be. Orwell is especially interesting in this regard: he craves the idea of an English national character, but cannot quite convince himself that it exists:

> It is not easy to discover the connecting thread that runs through English life from the sixteenth century onwards, but all English people who bother about such subjects feel that it exists... The belief that we resemble our ancestors may be unreasonable, but by existing it influences conduct. Myths which are believed in tend to become true, because they set up a type, or 'persona', which the average person will do his best to resemble.[25]

But what is this English national persona? The overwhelming self-image is of an essentially benign people inclined to hold their peace and to live and let live. Cyril Connolly wrote of the 'stolid, practical, tolerant, pleasure-loving, responsibility-taking English character'.[26] Lord Reith defined it through 'democracy, tolerance and kindliness'.[27] Orwell wrote of 'the gentle-mannered, undemonstrative, law-abiding English' and 'the orderly behaviour of English crowds, the lack of pushing and quarrelling, the willingness to form queues, the good temper of harassed, overworked people, like bus conductors'.[28] But he was also aware that 'this gentleness of manners is a recent thing' and that 'well within living memory... an eminent jurist, asked to name a typically English crime, could answer "Kicking your wife to death".'[29]

It is, moreover, not at all clear *to whom* English tolerance and kindliness can and cannot be extended. The Irish playwright John B. Keane, a typical unskilled migrant of the mid-1950s, remembered his landlady Beryl Atkinson and her husband Henry in Northampton. 'Like most of the houses on the street, hers had a notice in the window warning "No negroes, no Irish", with *"This means you Paddy!"* in italics underneath.' Keane persuaded her that he was Scottish and was taken in as a boarder. Beryl was furious when she discovered the truth: 'You told me you was Jocks when you was downright Paddies all along. I'm not 'avin' no Paddies in this 'ouse. It says so on my window.' Yet Keane was still struck by the basic goodness of the Atkinsons: 'Beryl was a scrupulously honest woman. She was no exception as far as most English landladies went. 'Enery, as we called him, was fair and decent.'[30]

This is emblematic of all notions of character, individual and collective – fairness, decency and tolerance are not indivisible. 'Character' holds out the promise of a solid substratum of attitudes and manners that can underpin a workable collective identity. It matters a great deal to English people: asked to name two things that symbolize their identity, English respondents chose a 'sense of fair play' (41 per cent) far ahead of the Union Jack (27 per cent) or 'God Save the Queen' (11 per cent).[31] But this is a promise that cannot be fulfilled. 'Character' is neither singular nor stable. 'Undemonstrative' and 'stolid' Englishness, if it ever existed, was drowned in the hot tears of Princess Diana's death in 1997, a moment of national nervous breakdown that now seems, in its festive self-pity and inchoate rage at the British state, like a strange preview of Brexit. (It was then that the English flag of St George began to displace the Union Jack in a non-sporting arena.)

And, returning to the same Northampton of John B. Keane's Beryl and 'Enery, one of its native sons, Jeremy Seabrook, lamented in 1996 that

> all those characteristics, the self-flattering myths with which Britain has consoled itself – our unique tolerance and good humour, our sympathy with the underdog, our fair-mindedness and sense of justice – have been violently discon-firmed. It is clear that we have become less tolerant, that we celebrate power and wealth with a fawning sycophancy that makes even archaic deference to birth and breeding appear modest and reasonable. Our love of fair play has turned into nice work if you can get it. As for the underdogs, we regularly step over their bodies sprawled on the sidewalk. We are xenophobic, unjust and unkind…[32]

This gloomy vision may be no more a fixed truth than the self-flattering myths ever were, but what is undoubtedly true is that the smashing of working-class communities under Thatcherism could not have left even those myths intact.

What remains of 'character', though, are two toxic notions, both of which are in the very bloodstream of Brexit. Firstly, if you insert the indefinite article, you get 'a character', also known as an eccentric. The idea of eccentricity – though closely hedged in by class and gender – has a long history as a signifier of English freedom. England's glorying in upper-class eccentrics, so the story went, contrasted favourably with the conformism of slavish continentals and was thus a kind of personal tribute to the virtues of the constitution. But it was meant to be free of damage – the invariable modifier of 'eccentric' was 'harmless'. And so it was: when your ruling class is running a vast empire and your practical industrialists are leading the world, you can afford a decorative eccentric or two.

England can no longer afford an eccentric ruling class, but this is one area in which deficit spending has gone wild. In characters like Boris Johnson and Jacob Rees-Mogg, the old English indulgence of eccentricity has been grafted onto the mass-media cult of celebrity and a broad revolt against colourless identikit career politicians to create an invasive species as tenacious and damaging as Japanese knotweed. The harm*ful* eccentric is a construct to which the very English language seems resistant. But the harm is all too real: the indulgence of eccentricity brought clownish absurdity and self-centred recklessness into the heart of political power. Figures who would have been enjoyably ridiculous in a Dickens novel now get to determine a nation's fate for a generation.

The other toxic waste from the faded myths of English character is pain-as-redemption. It harks back to the grand heroic failures, to the doomed youth of the First World War, to Dunkirk and the Blitz. But John Major, when he was imposing austerity as Margaret Thatcher's chancellor in 1990, gave it a very particular politico-economic twist: 'If it isn't hurting, it isn't working.'[33] It is easy to see what this will become as Brexit unfolds: it is working *because* it is hurting. While all rational political discourse would say 'this is a bad idea, it is causing great suffering', we will hear instead 'this great suffering is the proof that we were right'. On the lunatic fringe of Brexit – a fringe long enough to get in the eyes of rational governance – there is a belief that England can find itself only when the remnants of socialism and liberalism are burned off in the crucible of pain. Suffering is not a side effect of the great project; it *is* the medicine.

Whatever happens with Brexit, this toxic sludge will be in England's political groundwater for a long time. The self-pity of Lost Causism will meld with the rage of betrayal. Without the EU as whipping boy and scapegoat, there will be no end of blame and no shortage of candidates to be saddled with it: anyone and everyone except the Brexiteers themselves. That most virulent of poisons, the 'stab-in-the-back', is in the bloodstream now and it will work its harm for a long time.

Unless there is an antidote. Can one be found? The first place to look might be to return to the sore tooth. I have suggested that Brexit is a radical operation on the wrong part of the body. It does not in fact address the deep but unsettled sense of an emergent English political community that helped to make it happen. If this is true, then precisely this task remains to be fulfilled. And it does not have to be done from the reactionary right. It does not have to be a vehicle for the completion of the neoliberal capture of English society, or for a nasty and paranoid authoritarianism, or for the feckless self-interest of a small bunch of chancers. There is nothing innately shameful about the idea of England as a distinct political community

– why should it not be one? Indeed, it is perfectly possible to see the re-emergence of England as the final stage in the dismantling of Empire. What folded itself into the imperial construct must eventually unfold again.

One of the side effects of Brexit is to make progressives recoil even further from English nationalism, which they never trusted and now blame for the disaster. But they need to do what they mostly did not do in the pre-Brexit decade: take it seriously. Address it. Precisely because it remains so poorly articulated and self-contradictory, it is up for grabs. And there is surely enough in the English radical, socialist and liberal traditions – the traditions of John Ball and the Suffragettes, of Mary Wollstonecraft and John Maynard Keynes, of Stuart Hall and Thomas Paine, of Jo Cox and George Orwell and generations of fighters for dignity and equality – to inspire a more positive sense of national belonging. There is surely, in one of the world's great cultures, enough wit and energy and creativity and humour to infuse Englishness with hope and joy instead of pain and self-pity.

'Perhaps,' thinks Edward St Aubyn's Patrick Melrose as he tries to imagine a future beyond self-destruction, 'that's all identity is: seeing the logic of our own experience and being true to it.'[34] Self-harm is surely not the only logic of England's experience.

And as well as the sore tooth, there is the broken umbrella. A nation state is, first and foremost, a shelter. In the hard rain of neoliberal globalization, people know that they cannot be fully protected. But they do reasonably expect an umbrella over their heads. The problem is that the umbrella is broken, its material tattered, its struts sticking out like bared bones. The welfare state that kept self-pity at bay has been relentlessly undermined. Its basic promise – security against poverty and indignity – is, for too many, hollow. Brexit is part of a much larger phenomenon and it speaks to two much wider truths. One is that it is not possible simultaneously to ask people to trust the state and to tell them that the state has no business in any part of their lives in which the market wants free rein. The other is that the gross inequality produced by neoliberalism is increasingly incompatible with democracy and therefore, in liberal democracies, with political stability. If there is to be a world beyond pain and self-pity, it is necessary to fix the umbrella.

8.

POSTSCRIPT:
A SPECIAL PLACE IN HELL

It was a bright cold day in April,
and the clocks were striking thirteen

— GEORGE ORWELL, *1984*

O n 18 January 2019, just ten weeks before the date Britain
had chosen as its last day in the European Union, the
historian Sir Anthony Seldon arrived at 10 Downing
Street, the prime minister's official residence in London. He
carried with him some documents from the National Archives,
of which he is chairman. Among them was a detailed map of
the battle of Rorke's Drift, fought during the Zulu wars in
1879, drawn by one of its leading participants, Lieutenant John
Chard. The encounter occurred in the immediate aftermath
of the defeat of the British by the Zulus at Isandlwana. It was
of limited military importance, but the successful defence of a
small mission station by a tiny British force against a massively

larger Zulu army provided imaginative compensation for Isandlwana. The real failure in the big battle became, at Rorke's Drift, heroic. As we have seen, the movie that plays on the hotel TV in the first episode of *Patrick Melrose*, while Patrick is having his breakdown, is *Zulu*, which depicts this great drama of British pluck alchemically transmuting disaster into triumph.

The *Sunday Times* reported of Seldon's visit to Theresa May's Downing Street staff that 'The embattled aides, outnumbered and seemingly under attack from all sides, drew strength' from poring over Chard's map. 'Those looking for hope see May as a latter-day Lieutenant Chard, rallying her troops.'[1] The article was illustrated with images of red-coated, pith-helmeted British soldiers dressed like Stanley Baker and Michael Caine in *Zulu*, but with the faces of May, Michael Gove and other members of the cabinet superimposed on them.

A week later, now with just nine weeks to go to 29 March, Tom Enders, chief executive of one of the most important manufacturers in Britain, the pan-European aircraft maker Airbus, issued an open letter to warn that the company, its workers and suppliers stood 'on the edge of a precipice' because of 'the Brexiteers' madness'. Airbus provides, directly and indirectly, 124,000 jobs in the UK. Their loss would be catastrophic for many communities in England, Scotland, Wales and Northern Ireland. But Enders, as it happens, is German. So a Conservative MP stood in front of the Houses of Parliament in Westminster and tore up a copy of his open letter on live TV. Mark Francois, a prominent member of the cabal of ultra-Brexiteers led by Jacob Rees-Mogg that calls itself the European Research Group (ERG), told the BBC that 'Mr

Enders' intervention is a classic example of the sort of Teutonic arrogance which is one of the reasons why many people voted to leave the European Union . . . My father Reginald Francois was a D-Day veteran. He never submitted to any bullying by any German. Neither will his son. So if Mr Enders is watching, that's what he can do with his letter.'[2] He also claimed that Enders was 'a German paratrooper in his youth'.

On 30 January, when the Brexit deadline was six days closer still, there was another strange emanation from the English historical unconscious. On the BBC's six o'clock TV news, the anchor Sophie Raworth was telling viewers that 'Theresa May says she intends to go back to Brussels to negotiate her Brexit deal but EU leaders say the deal is done and they will not reopen talks.' But behind her, the screen showed a squadron of Second World War–era planes taking off from the RAF's Biggin Hill base. The base, just twelve miles from London, had been crucial during another episode in which the British fought off enemies against seemingly overwhelming odds, the Battle of Britain in 1940. Today, it offers tourists the chance to see restored Spitfires, a Hurricane and a German Messerschmitt 109e. The programme's editor blamed 'simple human error' and reassured viewers that it was 'pretty certain' May was 'not travelling to Brussels like this'.[3]

The next day, at a meeting in Westminster of the anti-European Bruges Group presided over by Rees-Mogg, an elderly gentleman named Max Gammon made a passionate speech in which he claimed: 'Brexit is presented primarily as a matter of economics, rather than as a struggle for freedom from bondage to a dictatorial continental oligarchy. We have been given a picture of a negotiation between friends and partners. But we are in fact at war.' And in this rerun of the Second World War, 'our enemies abroad and at home are winning while we are in shameful retreat'.[4]

And on 11 February, with just forty-six days to go before the Brexit deadline, the UK's actual secretary of state for defence, Gavin Williamson, made a major speech on his government's long-term military strategy: 'As we leave the European Union... it is up to us to seize the opportunities that Brexit brings... We should be the nation that people turn to when the world needs leadership... The UK is a global power with truly global interests... Some still wish to cut Britain down to size and send her back to her shores. But to those I say that has never been our way. It is not in our nature... Brexit has brought us to a moment. A great moment in our history. A moment when we must strengthen our global presence, enhance our lethality, and increase our mass.' As well as enhancing its lethality, increasing its mass and extending beyond its own island shores, the global power that post-Brexit Britain was about to become would establish new permanent military bases 'in areas including the Caribbean and Asia–Pacific to extend our global influence'.[5] In Williamson's head at least, Britain was about to regain the Great Power status it had lost in the Suez crisis of 1956.

Three days after the conjuring of this neo-imperial phantasm, now with just forty-three days left until the Brexit deadline, another Conservative MP, Robert Halfon, rose in the House of Commons to demand an official government statement on a matter of extreme urgency: 'May we have a statement on the achievements of the former MP for Harlow and Epping between 1924 and 1945?' The former MP in question was Winston Churchill, and Halfon wished the House to note that he was 'not only our greatest Prime Minister but a wonderful social reformer and the man who defeated Nazi tyranny'.[6] His request was welcomed by the leader of the House, Andrea Leadsom. No one intervened to suggest that the parliament of a country on the brink of a momentous disruption might have more urgent things to discuss.

By this time, the first ships had already sailed from Britain to destinations they would reach only after 29 March. From 8 February, freighters leaving UK ports for Australia and New Zealand were sailing into the unknown. Their voyage would take fifty days, so they would arrive after the Brexit deadline. Which meant that they had departed with no idea of what trading regime would apply when they tried to land their goods. From 15 February, the same became true of ships leaving Britain for ports in Asia. In their own weird way, these voyages were replicating the conditions of heroic and frequently disastrous eighteenth-century imperial explorations, turning many British sea captains into descendants of Captain Cook.

These stout mariners may have known where they were going in a literal sense, but they had no idea what awaited them. Quarantine? Tariffs? Demands for papers they did not have? They had left a place of legal certainty and were going into the trading equivalent of terra incognita. Of the trade arrangements with sixty-nine non-European countries the UK enjoyed through its membership in the EU, just seven had been replaced by this time – the rest could have lapsed before the ships tried to tie up in port. These were Brexit's ghost ships, floating away into some strange liminal zone.

What we glimpse in these moments is that, with Brexit, time was out of joint. Britain simultaneously occupied two completely different temporal worlds. In one, Brexit was hurtling ever faster forward, towards a known and supposedly unbreakable appointment with fate. Not just known but chosen. It was entirely a matter for the British to start the timer, to say to their imagined destiny, as in an old-fashioned romantic movie: let's make a date to meet under the clock at 11 p.m. on 29 March 2019. The very hour was specified in law. And it was supposed to be irrevocable. When Theresa May triggered the legal mechanism for exiting the EU, Article 50 of the Lisbon Treaty, she told parliament that 'there can be no turning back'.

And yet, there was nothing but turning back. In any rational process, the two years allowed for Britain to negotiate a withdrawal agreement with Brussels would have been a time of urgency and immediacy. The country had twenty-four months in which to undo nearly half a century of profound legal, economic and political entanglement with the EU. This was also the biggest constitutional change in the nature of the UK since Irish independence in 1922. Even if Brexit were a good idea, it was obviously an immense task. Each of the 730 available days mattered, and one might have expected British hearts to beat faster as each one of them was marked off on the calendar.

But there was instead a strange meandering, every movement towards a feasible agreement followed by a looping back into previously discarded impossibilities. Take the most notorious example, the 'backstop' agreement to ensure that whatever final trading arrangements might be agreed between the UK and the EU, the Irish border would remain open and invisible. It was agreed formally by Theresa May in December 2017, contradicted by some of her ministers in the following weeks, agreed again by May in March 2018 in a draft withdrawal agreement, included in the final withdrawal agreement in November 2018, effectively repudiated by May in January 2019 and then tentatively embraced again as government policy.

It made a weird kind of sense that the conundrum of the Irish backstop resolved itself into an argument about temporal states: was it to be 'temporary', as the Brexiteers wanted, or 'indefinite', as the Irish and Europeans demanded? On the difference between the temporary and the indefinite, real time – the scarce time for negotiation – was wasted, the same argument endlessly rehearsed, resolved and reopened. Groundhog Day may be an American notion, but the British created a Bulldog Day with the same meaning. The linear time of the countdown to 29 March functioned only for the Europeans – for the British, it seemed, all the timelines were loops.

This loopiness was inherent in Brexit itself. On the surface, it proposed a linear historical motion: from the 'then' of 1973–2019, when Britain was in the EU, to the 'now' of the moment of destiny on 29 March, when it entered a new phase of being, to the future state after liberation when Global Britain would re-emerge to lead the world again. But not very far beneath the surface was the illusion that the new 'now' would still have all the good things from 'then'. Brexit was simultaneously imagined as both a decisive break from the past and an easy continuation of it.

This was the essence of the 'have cake/eat cake' fantasy. And its proponents were not just on the Right. The then–Brexit secretary David Davis told the House of Commons in January 2017 that 'What we have come up with ... is the idea of a comprehensive free trade agreement and a comprehensive customs agreement that will deliver the exact same benefits as we have.' The opposition Labour Party then laid down six tests for what an acceptable Brexit would look like, and one of them explicitly echoed Davis: 'Does it deliver the "exact same benefits" as we currently have as members of the Single Market and Customs Union?'[7]

In a narrow tactical sense, this was smart politics – taking an absurd promise on its own terms and then using it as a weapon against a government that could not possibly fulfil it. But as a broader strategy, it was disastrous. It meant that the leadership of both main parties kept alive the fantasy that all would change and nothing would change, that 29 March would be at once a defining date with destiny and a casual hook-up over a shared love of cake. It also meant that the primary political opposition was caught in a state of self-induced paralysis, willing neither to oppose Brexit itself nor to accept what, in the real world, it would actually look like: a voluntary swapping of first-class membership in the EU for a subordinate, second-class membership. Both main British parties were thus unable to articulate a tangible sense of the 'before' and 'after', clear neither about the supposed wrongs of the previous forty-five years of EU membership nor about the future that lay beyond 29 March 2019.

In this temporal equivalent of no-man's-land, time was both scarce and plentiful. Since everything was about to change, the days leading up to the point of no return were short and few. Since everything was going to be 'the exact same', the days were long and many. In one time frame, an agreement had to be made and stuck to, contingency plans had to be laid in case of failure, a whole society had to be prepared for a momentous change in its place in the world. In the other, there was no need to do anything much except wait. For what? For that most radiant point in time: the last moment.

The idea of what would happen at the last moment was shaped by the belief among English reactionaries that the EU is really nothing more than a front behind which lurks the reality of German domination. It followed from this article of faith that all the tedious negotiations with Brussels were a sham. In the end – the very end – if Britain stood firm and held its nerve, the Germans, terrified of a no-deal Brexit, would abandon the pretense that the other twenty-six EU member states (least of all Ireland) mattered. The real deal would be done in Berlin and it would be tremendous because, in this test of character against Germany, England would have won again as it had always won before. This is essentially what Davis argued after the withdrawal agreement – so painfully concluded between Theresa May and the EU after two years of negotiations – was overwhelmingly rejected by the House of Commons in January 2019: 'The truth is now coming home to roost for Angela Merkel. I've always said that the Germans would sit it out and see who blinks first. It's plain as a pikestaff – if it's coming down to no deal, they'll renegotiate, either before 29 March or shortly afterwards.'[8]

Note here that 'they' are the Germans. This is 'the truth' about the EU and it will lead to Brexit's own great moment of truth. But note also that the moment of truth may well be after the last moment of 29 March. Beyond the end point of the process, beyond the point of no return, there is a perfect Brexit deal. Which forces the question: what time will it be when this happens? And the obvious Orwellian answer: it will be thirteen o'clock on a bright, cold day in April 2019 – a fateful hour that, of course, never came.

There is a deeper reason for the extraordinary inability of the Brexit process to keep within the time frame it created for itself, for the loopiness that made a rational process of negotiation and settlement so extremely difficult. There is constant interference from another channel that plays on a loop old pseudo-historical movies about Zulus and Spitfires and Germans and the resurrection of Britain's global power. It is the dreamtime that this book has sketched, full of old junk left over by Empire and the Second World War.

And full too of the self-pity generated by a conviction that Britain deserves everything from Europe and is getting nothing. The pro-Brexit Tory MP Daniel Kawczynski tweeted on 2 February 2019, in a rage that the EU was refusing to give Britain everything it wants: 'Britain helped to liberate half of Europe. She mortgaged herself up to eye balls in process. No Marshall Plan for us only for Germany. We gave up war reparations in 1990. We put £370 billion into EU since we joined. Watch the way ungrateful EU treats us now. We will remember.' But this is not remembering – it is forgetting. Britain in fact received more than 25 per cent of the $12 billion in aid from the US for the rebuilding of post-war Europe, almost twice as much as Germany did. Kawczynski refused to withdraw the claim when its inaccuracy was pointed out, and in a way he was right not to do so. For he was evoking not a set of facts about the past but that much deeper sense of the contrast, described by Herbert Spencer, between the sufferer's 'own worth as he estimates it and the treatment he has received'.

Within this pseudo-historical dreamtime, it is impossible to imagine Brexit as what it is supposed to be: a departure. Take a very simple idea about what would happen in Britain after its liberation. At the Conservative Party conference in September 2018, Theresa May announced that there would be a great Festival of Great Britain and Northern Ireland in 2022 to mark the end of the transition period after Brexit and the beginning of the new era. This would be problematic in itself, since neither Scotland nor Northern Ireland actually voted for Brexit and might well therefore be found wanting when it came to the celebration of their new-found freedom from European tyranny. But the festival would nevertheless mark the advent of a supposed new political order.

Except that May explicitly framed the 2022 national rejoicing as a revisiting of the 1951 Festival of Britain: 'Almost 70 years ago, the Festival of Britain stood as a symbol of change. Britain once again stands on the cusp of a new future as an outward-facing, global trading nation. Just as millions of Britons celebrated their nation's great achievements in 1951, we want to showcase what makes our country great today.'⁹ The 'symbol of change' to inaugurate a 'new future' must be understood as a replaying of the past – and not just of any past but of the immediate post-war period.

When European Council President Donald Tusk, in a carefully planned expression of spontaneous exasperation, claimed on 6 February 2019 that 'I've been wondering what that special place in Hell looks like, for those who promoted Brexit without even a sketch of a plan how to carry it out safely', he was probably thinking only of the place in Hell, not of what would be special about it. But Brexit is a Dantesque kind of Inferno, one in which each great sinner has a bespoke kind of punishment. The particular torment that Brexit inflicts on its country is a paradox of duration. Its fate is both to vanish instantly and to last forever, to be both past and future, to recede in the rear-view mirror and to loom ever ahead.

The special place in Hell is really a special time. Brexit, from the moment of its triumph on 23 June 2016, was always already finished. It was dead on arrival. The 'ex' was built in: it could not survive its victory because victory moved it from the invented to the real, from the struggle against imaginary oppression to the impossibility of freeing yourself from non-existent tyranny. Brexit was always a project that could not survive contact with reality. From the moment it was born, it was always going to be, in the minds of its supporters, something that might have been – if only. If only the Europeans had not been so pig-headed; if only the Irish had not been so troublesome; if only the enemy within had not been so traitorous; if only everyone had simply believed strongly enough.

But alongside this instant ex-Brexit, there runs what forty former senior British ambassadors and high commissioners called, in an open letter in February 2019, 'a "Brexternity" of endless uncertainty about our future'.[10] Brexit is in the past but it is not over. No one can really imagine a post-Brexit Britain, partly because the upheaval has made it impossible to be confident that the UK will continue to exist as a political entity and partly because, however it unfolds, its long-term consequences will be as profound as they are unknowable. All that can be said is what Mary Tyrone says in that other *Long Day's Journey into Night*: 'The past is the present, isn't it? It's the future, too.' Brexit is the afterlife of dead fantasies, but afterlives can continue for a very long time.

Ironically, this drama of departure has really served only to displace a crisis of belonging. Brexit is rooted in a supposed conflict between Them and Us, but it was surely obvious after almost three years of paralysis that the problem is not with Them on the European continent. It is with the 'British' Us, the unravelling of the imagined community of the UK under the pressure of a rising but incoherent English nationalism. The visible collapse of the Westminster polity – with a prime minister in office but patently not in power and the two-party system moving far beyond its breaking point – may have been a result of Brexit. But Brexit itself is the result of the invisible subsidence of the British political order over recent decades.

It may seem strange to call this slow collapse 'invisible',

since so much of it is obvious: the deep uncertainties about the Union after the Belfast Agreement of 1998 and the establishment of the Scottish parliament the following year; the consequent rise of English nationalism; the profound regional and social inequalities within England itself; the generational divergence of values and aspirations; the undermining of the welfare state and its promise of shared citizenship; the contempt for the poor and vulnerable expressed through a decade of austerity; the emergence of a sensationally self-indulgent and clownish ruling class. But the collective effects of these interrelated developments do seem to have been barely visible within the political mainstream until David Cameron accidentally took the lid off by calling a referendum and asking people, in effect, to endorse the status quo.

What we have seen with the lid off is the truth that Brexit is much less about Britain's relationship with the EU than it is about Britain's relationship with itself. It is the projection outwards of an inner turmoil. An archaic political system had carried on even while its foundations in a collective sense of belonging were crumbling. Brexit in one way alone has done a real service: it has forced the old system to go through its death throes in public. The spectacle is ugly, but at least it shows that a fissiparous four-nation state cannot be governed without radical political, social and constitutional change.

A part of that process of change must be a search for a more open sense of Englishness. It is striking that, in one study a decade before Brexit, 75 per cent of English respondents said that more should be done to celebrate St George's Day as an English national holiday in the way the Irish mark St Patrick's

Day. Yet 72 per cent said they had absolutely no plans to celebrate St George's Day themselves.[11] Nearly half said they would like people to fly the English flag but only 11 per cent said they would do so themselves. These findings are relatively unimportant in themselves, but they do point to a deeper unease: Englishness was being felt as something that 'should be' expressed, but not as something that one can express oneself. What has happened since is that the imperative to express it has become overwhelming, Brexit being in part the result. But there is still very little actual self-expression involved: Brexit did not really give voice to an emerging English national sense of belonging.

There is still, to return to Johnny Rotten, no future in England's dreaming. This is why, as Andrew Cooper, a former adviser to the British government, put it, 'There's no such thing as post-Brexit, I think it will define us for the rest of our lives.'[12] An appeal to the plucky English ability to endure pain must wear thin when the pain is self-inflicted. A tragi-comic self-parody of an Englishness that draws on distorted memories of the Second World War, strange reversals of imperial attitudes and recycled myths of heroic failure cannot perform an exit. Brexit will always be like the end of Samuel Beckett's *Waiting for Godot*, in which Vladimir asks: 'Well, shall we go?' and Estragon answers: 'Yes, let's go.' The stage direction is 'They do not move.'

In order to move, England has to move on. It has to dismantle the archaic political system that effectively disenfranchises millions of voters, to rid itself of the vestiges of feudalism, to genuinely allow communities to 'take back control' of their lives. It has to re-animate the spirit of social reform that created its great liberal and social democratic movements. It has to re-invent the egalitarianism that has been undermined so thoroughly since the Thatcherite revolution. It has to learn something from the way the other nationalisms on the islands it shares – Scottish, Irish and Welsh – have tried to articulate a civic belonging that is open, multi-layered and, yes, European. It has to discover the future tense.

European leaders continually expressed exasperation that, in the Brexit talks, the British had really been negotiating not with them but with each other. But perhaps there is a useful truth in this: Brexit is really just the vehicle that has delivered a fraught state to a place where it can no longer pretend to be a settled and functioning democracy. It is time to move on from the pretense that the problem with British democracy is the EU and to recognise that its primary problem is with itself. If there is ever to be a time after Brexit, it will come when the people who share the current British state really do begin to negotiate with each other, collectively and honestly, who they are and where they belong.

Notes

Preface: The Importance of Not Being Earnest

1 Kate Fox, *Watching the English: The Hidden Rules of English Behaviour*, revised edition, Hodder & Stoughton, London, 2014, pp. 83–84.

2 Ibid., p. 85.

3 Ibid., p. 87.

4 'Theresa May should have taken my father's advice on Brexit,' by Donald Trump Jr, *Daily Telegraph*, 19 March 2019.

1. The Pleasures of Self-Pity

1 Leigh Hunt, *Selections from the English Poets*, Philadelphia, 1856, p. 245.

2 Herbert Spencer, *The Principles of Psychology*, Vol. 2, London, 1872, p. 591.

3 Colin Wilson in Going into Europe – Again? A Symposium, *Encounter*, July 1971, pp. 18–32.

4 Arnold Toynbee, 'Saving England', *Encounter*, January 1962.

5 James Morris, 'Patriotism', *Encounter*, January 1962, p. 17.

6 Clive Archer, *The European Union*, Routledge, 2008, p. 24.

7 Matthew Connolly (ed.), *The Selected Works of Cyril Connolly*, Vol. 1, Picador, London, 2002, p. 343.

8 *Encounter*, January 1962, p. 18.

9   Going into Europe – Again? A Symposium, *Encounter*, June 1971, pp. 3–17.

10 Ibid., pp. 18–32.

11 Ibid.

12 Richard Weight, *Patriots: National Identity in Britain 1940–2000*, Macmillan, London, 2002, p. 521.

13 *Encounter*, June 1971, pp. 3–17.

14 Linda Colley, *Captives: Britain, Empire and the World, 1600–1850*, Jonathan Cape, London, 2002, p. 376.

15 White Paper, The United Kingdom and the European Communities, July 1971, p. 2.

16 Jean Rook, *Daily Express*, January 1, 1973.

17 *Encounter*, July 1971, pp. 18–32.

18 Ibid.

19 Ibid., pp. 3–17.

20 Ibid.

21 White Paper, 1971, p. 17.

22 *Encounter*, June 1971, pp. 3–17.

23 Ibid.

24 Ibid., pp. 18–32.

25 Weight, *Patriots*, p. 46.

26 Francis Wheen, *Hoo-hahs and Passing Frenzies: Collected Journalism, 1991–2001*, Atlantic Press, London, 2002, p. 92.

27 Francis Wheen, *Strange Days Indeed: The Golden Age of Paranoia*, Fourth Estate, London, pp. 51–2.

28 Weight, *Patriots*, p. 514.

29 Arnold Toynbee, 'Saving England', *Encounter*, January 1962, pp. 7–8.

30 Camilla Schofield, *Enoch Powell and the Making of Postcolonial Britain*, Cambridge University Press, Cambridge, 2013, pp. 8, 231.

31 Jane Gardam, *Old Filth*, Abacus, London, 2005, p. 56.

2. SS-GB: Life in Occupied England

1 Len Deighton, *SS-GB*, HarperCollins, London, 2009, p. 16.

2 Robert Harris, *Fatherland*, Arrow Books, London, 2012, p. 14.

3 Anthony Barnett, *The Lure of Greatness*, Unbound, London, 2017, p. 278.

4 Jonathan Wright and Steven Casey (eds), *Mental Maps in the Era of Détente and the End of the Cold War, 1968–91*, Palgrave Macmillan, Basingstoke, 2015, p. 188.

5 Harris, *Fatherland*, p. 134.

6 Ibid., pp. 297–8.

7 Ibid., pp. 74–5.

8 Ibid., p. 288.

9 Ibid., p. 163.

10 Roger Helmer, tweet, 1 August 2018.

11 'Bruges groupies rally against '"Eurocracy"', by David Usborne, *Independent*, Saturday 22 April 1989, p. 12.

12 *Spectator*, 14 July 1990.

13 'Beleaguered Ridley expected to quit', by Anthony Bevins, *Independent*, Friday 13 July 1990, p. 1.

14 'Trail of disaster and indiscretion', by Peter Jenkins, ibid.

15 'Margaret lifts the lid off her larder', *Daily Express*, 29 November 1974.

16 Margaret Thatcher, Speech to Conservative Rally at Cheltenham, 3 July 1982, Margaret Thatcher Foundation, https://www.margaretthatcher.org/document/104989

17 Robert Saunders, *Yes to Europe! The 1975 Referendum and Seventies Britain*, Cambridge University Press, Cambridge, 2018, p. 19.

18 Mark Baimbridge (ed.) *The 1975 Referendum on Europe*, Vol. 1, *Reflections of the Participants*, Imprint Academic, Exeter, 2007, p. 14.

19 Saunders, *Yes to Europe!*, p. 16.

20 Ibid., pp. 25–7.

21 Quoted in Camilla Schofield, *Enoch Powell and the Making of Postcolonial Britain*, Cambridge University Press, Cambridge, 2013, p. 1.

22 Matthew Connolly (ed.), *The Selected Works of Cyril Connolly*, Vol. 1, Picador, London, 2002, p. 333.

23 Andrew Gilligan, 'The EU: so where did it all go wrong?', *Daily Telegraph*, 30 December 2012.

24 Boris Johnson, 'My vision for a bold, thriving Britain enabled by Brexit', *Daily Telegraph*, 15 September 2017.

25 John Newsinger, 'The Roast Beef of Old England', *International Journal of Health Services*, Vol. 27, No. 2, pp. 243–6, 1997.

26 'Germans urged to call truce in "mad cow" war', by Dennis Newson, *Daily Mail*, Wednesday 7 January 1990, p. 10.

27 'A small Somerset town finds itself at war with Germany, Beef Wellington at its Waterloo', *Daily Express*, 22 May 1996, p. 5.

28 *Daily Express*, 25 April 1996, p. 24.

29 'Sauerkraut', *The Times*, 26 March 1996, p. 18.

30 Newsinger, 'The Roast Beef of Old England'.

31 'Battle lines drawn for new beef war', by Sean Poulter, *Daily Mail*, 5 August 1999.

32 *Daily Mail*, 7 August 1999, pp. 12–13.

33 'Is there life outside?', by Michael Gove, *The Times*, 14 June 1996, p. 20.

34 Simon Heffer, *Daily Mail*, 23 December 1995, p. 11.

35 White Paper, 1971, pp. 4–5.

36 Ibid., pp. 7, 15.

37 'Continent is punishing us just because we're British', by Bernard Connolly, *Daily Express*, 25 April 1996.

38 *Encounter*, June 1971, pp. 3–17.

39 Richard Weight, *Patriots: National Identity in Britain 1940–2000*, Macmillan, London, 2002, p. 513.

40 Owen Sheers, *Resistance*, Faber e-book, 2011, p. 4.

41 Ibid., pp. 43, 50, 54, 121, 122.

42 C. J. Sansom, *Dominion*, Pan Books, London, 2013, pp. 41, 697–8.

43 *Daily Mail*, front page, 4 February 2017.

44 Arron Banks, *The Bad Boys of Brexit: Tales of Mischief, Mayhem & Guerrilla Warfare in the EU Referendum Campaign*, Biteback, London, 2016, p. 81.

45 Edward St Aubyn, *Some Hope*, Picador, London, 2012, p. 166.

46 Express online, Friday 17 November 2017.

47 Telegraph online, 6 November 2017.

48 Sun online, 16 November 2017.

49 Express online, 14 March 2018.

50 Daniel Hannan, tweet, 28 February 2018.

51 Ibid., 5.08 p.m., 29 July 2018.

52 Nick Boles, Telegraph online, 1 September 2018.

53 *Daily Telegraph*, 21 September 2018.

54 Ibid., 28 March 2018.

55 Ibid., 19 July 2018.

56 *Guardian*, 20 September 2018.

57 *Observer*, 23 September 2018.

58 *The Times*, 21 September 2018.

3. The Triumph of the Light Brigade

1 'Ship found in Arctic 168 years after doomed Northwest Passage attempt', by Paul Watson, *Guardian*, 12 September 2016.

2 Stephanie Barczewski, *Heroic Failure and the British*, Yale University Press, London, 2016, p. 59.

3 Ibid., p. 62.

4   Ibid., p. 65.

5   Ibid., p. 71.

6   Sherard Osborn, *Stray Leaves from an Arctic Journal*, London, 1852, p. 210.

7   Barczewski, p. 4.

8   Robert Falcon Scott, *Scott's Last Expedition*, London, 2011, p. 426.

9   Ibid., p. 100.

10 George Orwell, 'England Your England' in *The Lion and The Unicorn: Socialism and the English Genius*, in *Essays*, Everyman's Library, Knopf, New York, 2002, p. 296.

11 Ibid.

12 Kenneth Mahood cartoon, *Punch*, 6 February 1974, p. 212.

13 'Britain stands alone again, celebrating the myth of Dunkirk', by Robert Harris, *Sunday Times*, 27 May 1990.

14 'Fish, ferries and Agincourt', *The Economist*, 23 August 1980, p. 58.

15 'Island nation', by Brian Groom, *Financial Times*, 20 April 2010.

16 'We Shall Not Be Stopped', by Tom Hutchinson, *Daily Star*, 20 April 2010.

17 *Sunday Express*, 1 April 2012, p. 9.

18 'Jeremy Hunt warns EU a bad Brexit deal will stir Britain's "Dunkirk Spirit"', *Daily Telegraph*, 30 September 2018.

19 Quoted in Barczewski, *Heroic Failure and the British*, pp. 4–5.

20 Jane Gardam, *Old Filth*, Abacus, London, 2005, p. 242.

21 'Ministers aim to build "empire 2.0" with African Commonwealth', by Sam Coates and Marcus Leroux, *The Times*, 6 March 2017.

22 Kwasi Kwarteng, Priti Patel, Dominic Raab, Chris Skidmore and Elizabeth Truss, *Britannia Unchained: Global Lessons for Growth and Prosperity*, Palgrave Macmillan, Basingstoke, 2012, p. 1.

23 Ibid., p. 10.

24 Ibid., p. 61.

25 Ibid., p. 89.

26 Ibid., p. 10.

27 Ibid., p. 59.

28 Harold D. Clarke, Matthew Goodwin and Paul Whiteley, *Brexit: Why Britain Voted to Leave the European Union*, Cambridge University Press, Cambridge, 2017, pp. 175–6.

29 Edward St Aubyn, *Mother's Milk*, Open City Books, New York, 2005, pp. 147, 162.

30 C. J. Sansom, *Dominion*, Pan Books, London, 2013, pp. 9, 30, 686.

31 'Lord Nigel Lawson hopes Irish Republic realises its "mistake" and rejoins UK following Brexit', 24 February 2016, https://www.newstalk.com/Lord-Nigel-Lawson-hopes-Irish-Republic-realises-its-mistake-and-rejoins-UK-following-Brexit

32 *Irish Times*, 14 July 2018.

33 Quoted in Camilla Schofield, *Enoch Powell and the Making of Postcolonial Britain*, Cambridge University Press, Cambridge, 2013, p. 7.

34 Ibid., p. 7.

35 Ibid., p. 230.

36 Ibid., p. 20.

37 Ibid., p. 209.

38 http://www.euronews.com/2017/11/09/brexit-the-uk-would-be-an-eu-colony

39 https://www.bbc.com/news/av/uk-politics-42376559/jacob-rees-mogg-uk-must-not-be-eu-colony-after-brexit, 16 Dec 2017.

40 Daniel Hannan, tweet, 1 May 2018.

41 'Triumph of the Light Brigade', by Simon Edge, *Daily Express*, 23 October 2004, pp. 52–3.

4. **A Pint of Beer, a Packet of Prawn Cocktail Flavour Crisps and Two Ounces of Dog Shit, Please**

1   Boris Johnson, *Friends, Voters, Countrymen: Jottings on the Stump*, HarperCollins, London, 2002, p. 7.
2   Ibid., pp. 14–15.
3   'Johnson's "piccaninnies" apology', *Guardian*, 23 January 2008.
4   Camilla Schofield, *Enoch Powell and the Making of Postcolonial Britain*, Cambridge University Press, Cambridge, 2013, p. 233.
5   Michael Gove, 'Is there life outside?', *The Times*, 14 June 1996, p. 20.
6   Edward St Aubyn, *Some Hope*, Picador, London, 2012, p. 4.
7   George Orwell, 'The English People', in *Essays*, Everyman's Library, Knopf, New York, 2002, p. 610.
8   Thompson's essay is transcribed at https://againstreactionblog. wordpress.com/2017/08/28/going-into-europe-an-essay-by-e-p-thompson-1975/
9   'Eurobeer Menace', *Daily Mirror*, 25 June 1973.
10 'Your Shopping Basket and the Market', *Daily Mirror*, 30 May 1975.
11 Richard Weight, *Patriots: National Identity in Britain 1940–2000*, Macmillan, London, 2002, p. 514.
12 'That Tory "have cake and eat it" Brexit strategy explained in all its humiliating glory', by Dan Bloom, *Daily Mirror*, 29 November 2016.
13 'We'll Have Our Cake and Eat It', by Tom Newton-Dunn, *Sun*, 1 October 2016.
14 'Boris Johnson's top 50 quotes', by Alice Audley, *Daily Telegraph*, 18 June 2014.
15 Stanley Johnson, *Stanley, I Resume: Further Recollections of an Exuberant Life*, Biteback, London, 2014.
16 Richard Weight, *Patriots: National Identity in Britain 1940–2000*, Macmillan, London, 2002, p. 505.

17 'Boris in row over Jamie remarks', BBC News, 3 October 2006.

18 Robin Young, 'MEPs rally to defend flavoured crisps', *The Times*, 29 April 1991, p. 2.

19 'The nasty taste of Brussels directives', *Daily Mail*, 30 April 1991.

20 'I'm no longer Nasty, but please stop lying about Nice by Boris Johnson', *Daily Telegraph*, 17 October 2002.

21 Boris Johnson, *Friends, Voters, Countrymen*, pp. 218–19.

22 Ibid., p. 37.

23 'Great-uncle Ernest Thesiger's army camp', letter by John Thesiger, *Guardian*, 27 April 2014.

24 Edward St Aubyn, *Bad News*, Picador, London, 2012, p. 41.

25 Weight, *Patriots*, p. 724.

26 'Hunger for beef is a part of British pride', by Ross Benson, *Daily Express*, 30 March 1996, p. 11.

27 Christopher Hope, *Daily Telegraph*, 5 June 2018.

28 Jacob Rees-Mogg, 'My nanny made me the man I am', *Daily Telegraph*, 14 March 2014.

29 Alan Bennett, *Keep On Keeping On*, Farrar, Straus and Giroux, New York, 2016, p. 193.

30 Boris Johnson, *Friends, Voters, Countrymen*, p. 20.

31 Nigel Farage, tweet, 9 November 2017.

32 https://www.petebrown.net/2014/06/16/why-farages-foaming-pint-is-testamen/

33 Farming for the next generation: Secretary of State Michael Gove sets out his vision on the future of our farming industry at the Oxford Farming Conference 2018, published by DEFRA, 5 January 2018.

34 'If your child is fat then you are a bad parent', by Julia Hartley-Brewer, *Daily Telegraph*, 10 November 2015.

35 Tower Hamlets Police @MPSTowerHam, tweet, 3.10 p.m., 20 February 2018.

36 @GMPWhitefield, tweet, 10.49 p.m., 20 February 2018.

5. Sadopopulism

1 *Independent*, 27 March 2017.

2 Andrew Gimson, *Boris: The Adventures of Boris Johnson*, Simon & Schuster, London, pp. 111–12.

3 'Grundy Banned, *Today* team accused', *Guardian*, 3 December 1976.

4 *Great Interviews of the 20th Century*, *Guardian* booklet no. 8, 2007, p. 10. The interview was broadcast live on 1 December 1976.

5 Arron Banks, *The Bad Boys of Brexit: Tales of Mischief, Mayhem & Guerrilla Warfare in the EU Referendum Campaign*, Biteback, London, 2016, p. 3.

6 Malcolm McLaren in *Great Interviews of the 20th Century*, *Guardian* booklet no. 8, 2007, p. 15.

7 Ibid., p. 13.

8 Jon Savage, *Symbols Clashing Everywhere: Punk Fashion 1975–1980* in *Punk: Chaos to Couture*, Metropolitan Museum, New York, 2013, p. 26.

9 Ibid., p. 22.

10 Ibid., pp. 21–2.

11 Ibid., p. 26.

12 Malcolm McLaren in *Great Interviews of the 20th Century*, p. 14.

13 'Rusholme Ruffians', the Smiths, from *Meat is Murder*, 1985.

14 Nigel Farage, *The Purple Revolution: The Year that Changed Everything*, Biteback, London, 2016, p. 23.

15 Timothy Snyder, *The Road to Unfreedom*, Bodley Head, London, 2018, p. 273.

16 Harold D. Clarke, Matthew Goodwin and Paul Whiteley, *Brexit: Why Britain Voted to Leave the European Union*, Cambridge University Press, Cambridge, p. 186.

17 Banks, *The Bad Boys of Brexit*, p. 79.

18 Edward St Aubyn, *Bad News*, Picador, London, 2012, p. 95.

19 Craig Oliver, *Unleashing Demons, the Inside Story of Brexit*, Hodder & Stoughton, London, 2016, p. 100.

20 Richard Evans, '"One man who made history" by another who seems just to make it up: Boris on Churchill', *New Statesman*, 13 November 2014.

21 Treasury Committee oral evidence: The economic and financial costs and benefits of UK membership of the EU, HC 499, 23 March 2016.

22 Gimson, *Boris: The Adventures of Boris Johnson*, p. 121.

23 George Orwell, *Essays*, Everyman's Library, Knopf, New York, 2002, p. 149.

24 Ibid., p. 173.

25 Farage, *The Purple Revolution*, p. 26.

26 Peter Kellner, 'If so many Britons support freedom of movement, why doesn't Theresa May?', *Guardian*, 10 August 2018.

27 *Daily Mail*, 3 November 2016.

28 *Daily Mirror*, 17 May 2017.

29 *Daily Express*, 9 November 2016.

30 Ibid., 11 August 2017.

31 Ibid., 27 July 2018.

32 *Daily Telegraph*, 5 October 2016.

33 *The Shorter Oxford English Dictionary*.

6. The Twilight of the Gods: English Dreamtime

1 Edward St Aubyn, *Never Mind*, Picador, London, 2012, p. 17.

2 Jonathan Sumption, *Cursed Kings: The Hundred Years War*, Vol. IV, Faber & Faber, London, 2015, p. 374.

3 Gary Taylor, John Jowett and Terri Bourus and Gabriel Egan (eds), *The New Oxford Shakespeare*, Oxford University Press, Oxford, 2016, p. 1544.

4 Edward St Aubyn, *Some Hope*, Picador, London, 2012, pp. 126, 146.

5 'UK is a VASSAL state!', *Daily Express*, 12 July 2018.

6 'Boris Johnson's resignation speech in full: "It's not too late to save Brexit"', *Daily Telegraph*, 19 July 2018.

7   'Putin signals he will not back down over Ukraine', by Tom Parfitt, *Daily Telegraph*, 18 December 2014.

8   *Daily Express*, 8 February 2018.

9   *Daily Telegraph*, 23 August 2017.

10 'The Tory Three Brexiteers brandish boasts and the best gags', by Dan Roberts, *Guardian*, 3 October 2017.

11 Jonathan Sumption, *Trial by Battle: The Hundred Years War*, Vol. I, Faber & Faber, London, 1990, p. ix.

12 Ibid., p. 302.

13 Jonathan Sumption, *Trial by Fire: The Hundred Years War*, Vol. II, Faber & Faber, 1999, p. 494.

14 Ibid., p. 11.

15 Ibid., p. 438.

16 Ibid., p. 286.

17 Ibid., p. 434.

18 James Morris, *Encounter*, January 1962, p. 7.

19 Richard Weight, *Patriots: National Identity in Britain, 1940–2000*, Macmillan, London, p. 491.

20 Paul Readman, *Storied Ground: Landscape and the Shaping of English National Identity*, Cambridge University Press, Cambridge, 2018, p. 34.

21 Full Text: Boris Johnson's Brexit Speech, *Spectator*, 14 February 2018.

22 Arthur Koestler, Going into Europe – Again? A Symposium, *Encounter*, June 1971, pp. 3–17.

23 James Dale Davidson and Lord William Rees-Mogg, *The Sovereign Individual*, Touchstone, New York, 1999, p. 17.

24 Ibid., p. 21.

25 Ibid., p. 329.

26 Ibid., p. 32.

27 Ibid., p. 19.

28 Ibid., p. 20.

29 Ibid., pp. 196–7.

30 Ibid., p. 256.

31 Ibid., pp. 256–7.

32 Ibid., pp. 402–3.

33 Ibid., p. 129.

34 Ibid., p. 131.

35 'Why Silicon Valley billionaires are prepping for the apocalypse in New Zealand', by Mark O'Connell, *Guardian*, 15 February 2018.

36 *Irish Times*, 13 June 2018; 23 July 2018.

37 George Orwell, *Essays*, Everyman's Library, Knopf, New York, 2002, p. 164.

7. The Sore Tooth and the Broken Umbrella

1 Sarah Vine, 'Gosh, I suppose I better get up!', *Daily Mail*, 29 June 2016.

2 'The Spanish Job. Veteran actor Sir Michael Caine hails Brexit as The Sun tells Spain: "We only want to blow the bloody señors off"', Sun online, 6 April 2017.

3 *Encounter*, January 1962, p. 9.

4 James Shapiro, *1606: William Shakespeare and the Year of Lear*, Faber & Faber, London, 2015, pp. 48–9.

5 Richard Weight, *Patriots: National Identity in Britain, 1940–2000*, Macmillan, London, p. 731.

6 George Orwell, *Essays*, Everyman's Library, Knopf, New York, 2002, p. 608.

7 Institute for Public Policy Research (IPPR), *England and Its Two Unions: The anatomy of a nation and its discontents*, 2013, p. 7.

8 Institute for Public Policy Research (IPPR), *The Dog that Finally Barked: England as an emerging political community*, 2012, p. 19.

9 Ibid., p. 20.

10 Ibid., p. 14.

11 Ibid., p. 21.

12 Ibid., p. 31.

13 Ibid., p. 34.

14 Michael Kenny, *The Politics of English Nationhood*, Oxford University Press, Oxford, 2014, pp. 20–21.

15 Quoted in Anthony Barnett, *The Lure of Greatness*, Unbound, London, 2017, p. 115.

16 IPPR, *England and Its Two Unions*, p. 23.

17 Barnett, *The Lure of Greatness*, p. 123.

18 IPPR, *The Dog that Finally Barked*, p. 16; *England and Its Two Unions*, p. 18.

19 IPPR, *England and Its Two Unions*, p. 19.

20 Ibid., p. 22.

21 Harold D. Clarke, Matthew Goodwin and Paul Whiteley, *Brexit: Why Britain Voted to Leave the European Union*, Cambridge University Press, Cambridge, p. 167.

22 Jan Eichhorn, http://blogs.lse.ac.uk/politicsandpolicy/the-black-box-of-brexit-identification-with-englishness-is-the-best-clue/ 31 March 2018.

23 IPPR, *England and Its Two Unions*, p. 8.

24 Frank E. Vandiver, 'The Confederate Myth', in Patrick Gerster and Nicholas Cords (eds), *Myth and South History: The Old South*, Rand McNally, Chicago, 1974, p. 149.

25 Orwell, *Essays*, p. 613.

26 Matthew Connolly (ed.), *The Selected Works of Cyril Connolly*, Vol. 1, Picador, London, p. 344.

27 Quoted in Weight, *Patriots*, p. 40.

28 Orwell, *Essays*, pp. 613, 609.

29 Ibid., p. 610.

30 John B. Keane, *Self-Portrait*, Dublin and Cork, Mercier Press, 1964, pp. 42–3.

31 David McCrone and Frank Bechhofer, *Understanding National Identity*, Cambridge University Press, Cambridge, 2015, p. 175.

32 Jeremy Seabrook, 'An English Exile, in *Granta* 56: *What Happened to Us?*, Winter 1996, p. 188.

33 Robert Taylor, *Major*, Haus Publishing, London, 2016, p. 19.

34 Edward St Aubyn, *Some Hope*, Picador, London, 2012, p. 200.

Postscript: A Special Place in Hell

1 'Ready, aim, fire! May's troops wage battle of Downing Street', by Tim Shipman and Caroline Wheeler, *Sunday Times*, 20 January 2019.

2 BBC News Interview with Mark Francois, 25 January 2019, 12:09 p.m.

3 *Irish Times*, 31 January 2019.

4 Express online, 'We are at WAR': Brexiteer warns EU is 'intent on Britain's Brexit DEFEAT', 31 January 2019.

5 Defence in Global Britain, Transcript, https://www.gov.uk/government/speeches/defence-in-global-britain.

6 *Hansard Parliamentary Debates*, 14 February 2019.

7 The Labour Party, Theresa May's Failed Brexit Plan, September 2018, p. 4.

8 *Telegraph*, 17 January 2019.

9 *DailyMail.com*, 29 September 2019.

10 'Brexit is a national crisis, former diplomats tell Theresa May,' *Guardian*, 14 February 2019.

11 Kate Fox, *Watching the English*, revised edition, Hodder & Stoughton, London, 2014, p. 88.

12 Channel 4 News, 9 February 2019.

ABOUT THE AUTHOR

FINTAN O'TOOLE is a historian, biographer, literary critic and political commentator. His acclaimed columns on Brexit for the *Irish Times*, the *Guardian* and the *New York Review of Books* have been awarded both the Orwell Prize and the European Press Prize. His books include *A Traitor's Kiss*, his life of Richard Brinsley Sheridan, *Judging Shaw* and *White Savage*. His investigative, polemical books have all been bestsellers: *Meanwhile Back at the Ranch*, *Ship of Fools* and *Enough is Enough*. He is writing the authorised biography of Seamus Heaney and, for Head of Zeus, a history of Ireland in his own time.